MOSQUE
to the
CROSS

*Encountering God and
Hearing His Voice*

PASTOR ZAK GARIBA
Broadcast Host of "God Moments"

Legal Disclaimer

ISBN: 978-1-7774570-0-6
Published by: Pastor Zak Gariba

Gariba Ministries International
Visit us on the web: www.Gariba.org
Email: zkgariba@yahoo.ca or zak@gariba.org

I would like to dedicate this book to my Lord Jesus Christ, my Savior, whom I owe my life to. Without Him I would not be who I am today, so thank you.

To my beautiful wife, Pastor Karen-Marie, my life partner and friend for her patience, help, and support. To my dear son Zak Jr for being my assistant in so many ways and for coming up with the title of this book.

Also, to Geordie & Barbara Mundie, who have blessed me beyond measure, and who gave birth to the most wonderful person in my life Karen-Marie.

Also, to the memory of my mother in law Barbara Mundie who passed away on March 31, 2020 whom I had the privilege of knowing, I will never forget you.

And…

To the millions of readers who are going to come to faith or grow in their faith through this book.

Acknowledgements

Special appreciation and thanks goes to Karen-Marie, Zak Jr., Grant and Marilyn Holditch, and Kim Thompson-Pinder and her team at RTI Publishing, who have worked tirelessly and sacrificed so much of their time, advice to collaborate on and proofread the book.

I want to thank the following for their input, Jerry Steingard, Michael and Gerri Shortt, Jon and Lia Partridge, Bob and Kathy Shaw, June Welch and Diane Clark for their prayers and encouragement while writing this book.

I also want to thank my many friends and brothers and sisters in the Lord:

- Pastor Tony Soldano who is my prayer and accountability partner.

- The Moose Guys (Jerry Steingard, Al Remley, John Cook and Pastor Steve Barker) for their encouragement.

- Pastors Roger and Sheila Rayner who are friends and mentors.

- John and Patricia Bootsma for their mentorship.

- Pastor Barry Boucher for being a father in the Lord who believes in me.

- Steve Witt and Marc Dupont whom I look up to.

- Jamie and Christine Tonge

- Kenton and Ursula Baker

- My sisters-in-law Tracy and Cheryl who are incredible blessings.

- Joyce Chadwick, Isabel Allum, and Pastor Stephen and Amy Wong (from Taiwan) who have helped in shaping my life in so many ways.

- Janet Tonello Lakeside Graphics LakesideGraphics.ca

- Mel & Kae Campbell

Praise for Zak Gariba & *Mosque to the Cross*

Having known Zak and his ministry well for many years, I can authentically say that Zak is a practitioner of the gifts, not merely a teacher. I have been with Zak and the churches he oversees many times, and I have come to know that Zak lives what he preaches and teaches. I have found these churches to be easy places to minister at due to the continual emphasis and reliance on the Holy Spirit's leading and power! Mosque To The Cross will be a real encouragement as you journey with Christ and pursue His amazing presence!

- Marc Dupont, San Diego California, USA
www.marcdupontministries.org

Zak Gariba's life - from being groomed to be an Imam in his Nigerian birth country to becoming a pastor and prophetic voice from Canada to the nations - is nothing short of a miracle. I've known Zak from when he was a young man learning to walk with God to an anointed minister launching and pastoring numerous churches. Zak conveys the all-important Biblical truth that God prioritizes relationships over the ministry.

- Patricia Bootsma, Co-Sr. Leader Catch The Fire
USA, Author and Itinerant Minister

Does God still speak? Yes, He does! You can know His voice for yourself. In a world of many spiritual voices, Zak Gariba cuts through the noise and gets right to the heart of the matter—how to know God and His voice. There is no question that this man has had a first-hand encounter with Jesus, and that he speaks from a place of relational intimacy with God. Zak's life, integrity and ministry all come flooding through the pages of this book. His life is a testimony of the grace, power and incredible love of God. If God can do it for Zak Gariba, He can do it for you! Your eyes and heart will be opened to the truth. Your life is about to change!

- Rev. Dr. Tony Soldano, Lead Pastor All People's Church, Brampton, Canada

I absolutely love Zak Gariba's faith story. I am confident that through his journey shared in this enlightening book, that it will encourage you, and open your eyes to see what Jesus can do in a whole new way. The title of this book alone, should be enough to grab your attention.

- Shawn Gabie, Kingdom Culture Ministries, Ottawa, Canada

When I met Pastor Zak, his testimony broke open a fresh spring of love for Christ in my heart. The vision of Christ he shared with me melted me. His prophetic insight is trumped only by his love relationship with Christ. I want to encourage each reader to keep in their hearts the fact that the man who is writing this book has been with God, has seen the Lord and is anointed with Holy oil to minster the eternal into time.

- Eric Gilmour, Orlando Florida, USA

I know you will find his journey inspiriting, edifying, educational and it will inspire faith to pursue the things of God for your own life."

- Rev. Barry P Boucher, DMin, Life Centre, Ottawa

We have been so blessed by his ministry to our churches in Taiwan. He moves in the power of the Holy Spirit. I believe this book will be a blessing to many.

- Pastor Stephen Wong, Rehoboth Apostolic Holiness Church Taipei, Taiwan

I love Zak Gariba. He was one of the first prophets to actually prophesy a word into my life that changed me. I still remember it sixteen years later. He hears God's voice clearly, and this book is going to help you to process what God says to you. I encourage you to pick it up and read it because it will bless you abundantly.

- Darren Canning, Itinerary and Prophetic Minister

Do you want a very readable guide—a short yet sweeping overview of life in the Spirit for the new Christian—complete with prayers and contact support? This is it!

- Roger & Sheila Rayner, Prayer Counsellors Ottawa, Canada

Mosque to the Cross, by Pastor Zak Gariba, is not just an inspiring account of one man's miraculous journey into the heart of God, but it is a map for all of us to find a deeper more intimate relationship with Jesus.

- Joyce Chadwick, Director, Singing Waters Ministries

I highly recommend his ministry and his new book which tells some of his astounding personal testimony and offers real life stories that will inspire and stimulate your faith in a loving, communicating, supernatural God.

- Jerry Steingard, Lead Pastor Milverton Christian Fellowship

The principles he shares of intimacy with God are patterns that you can build your life upon. This is a must-read book for those seeking a dynamic relationship with God.

- Pastor Steve Barker, Hope Community Christian Church

I have watched him grow in accuracy and I have no doubt that he is tuned to the voice of the Lord. This book will be a great help to those who need to know that God still speaks today.

- Allen Remley, Founder of Forgotten People Connection a ministry to the forgotten people of the world.

Foreword

Seldom do you read a bold story like this. Its more than a story…it serves as a manual for total transformation. Zak's journey from Muslim Imam to Jesus follower to minister of the Gospel of Jesus Christ is an epic one.

Zak is a mover. He is loyal, committed and zealous for the things of God. He is deeply moved by supernatural evidence of the voice of God. He lives a life of intimacy with Jesus.

Like the Apostle Paul, he entered Christianity through a series of supernatural encounters. Paul was struck off his high horse of fundamental beliefs and turned into a healer rather than a destroyer. He needed time to absorb the shift but emerges as a preeminent apostle that travels the ancient world turning it upside down. God loves to use us all, regardless of our history and sometimes because of our history. Zak, like Paul has become a healer rather than a destroyer.

You will be reading about a man who has seen the presence of God and heard his voice. He has witnessed miracles and an alternate destiny than what he imagined as a young man. He doesn't stop there but leads the reader on a journey into the life of faith in Jesus. He functions like a tour guide, careful to answer your questions as the story unfolds. Prayers and guidance are offered to coach you into a deeper life.

I've known Zak for years and count him as a friend and fellow minister. I have watched him process questions that are on all of our minds. When resolve comes, action quickly follows. That's Zak. He is a man of faith. It has led him to build multiple church campuses in Canada and influence others internationally. He has remained somewhat hidden for a long time, but this book is a great introduction of an emerging man of faith that will mark the spiritual landscape of Canada and beyond.

Maybe you are hungry for God or have a Muslim friend that you'd love to understand and minister too? This book will guide you into a greater understanding and relationship with those of other faiths. The anointing on this book will empower you to move boldly and confidently to see a revival among Muslims across the world. Find a comfortable spot, get a coffee, and read away. You are likely to sense the same life changing revelations that came to Zak.

I love this man and his family and look forward to cheering in the bleachers as you discover the story that touched me and now will touch you. Be blessed in your pilgrimage!

Steve Witt

SteveWitt.com

Table of Contents

I have not spoken in secret,
In some dark land;
I did not say to the offspring of Jacob,
'Seek Me in a wasteland';
I, the LORD, speak righteousness,
Declaring things that are right.

Isaiah 45:19 NASB

Preface

*'Call to Me and I will answer you, and I will
tell you great and mighty things, which you do
not know.' Jeremiah 33:3 NASB*

I remember the first moment Jesus spoke to me. He came into my room beautiful, bright and shining. His love overwhelmed me as it flooded the room. I was overcome and could barely speak the words, "Who are you?" and He replied, "I am Jesus."

"What do you want from me?" "I love you. You are the reason I came and died on the cross. Will you follow Me?

Follow Him. What could I do? I felt dirty and unclean. I was a Muslim Imam, and I had hated Jesus all my life. Now He had appeared to me and told me He loved me. Jesus wiped the top of my head as He said, "You are no longer dirty, I have washed you clean. There is no more shame or guilt," and Jesus changed my life forever.

When God speaks, you are never the same.

Many people do not believe that God can or wants to speak to us anymore. Let me make it very clear from the start. God talks to us every day; it is we who do not know how to listen. His heart burns to have communication with us. He is a jealous Father who wants time with His kids. His love seeks us out. You accepted salvation because the Holy Spirit spoke to you first, and you responded.

The Time To Hear God Is Now

I wrote this book because you need to hear the Holy Spirit to live a good, wonderful, fulfilled life. If you cannot understand what He is saying, how can you follow Him?

The world we live in is filled with forces trying to deceive you and get you to turn away from God. They whisper things in your ear that you want to hear. They lie to you and promise you fake gold to draw you away from the Truth. Hearing God for yourself is the only way to stay strong in Him and successfully navigate life.

On the day you met Jesus, He uniquely spoke to you in a way that you could understand. God created each individual to hear Him uniquely, and there are things that only God can teach you.

The way He speaks to you is different than the way He speaks to me. Jesus takes the time to communicate uniquely to each person. Some people hear him audibly; some people hear Him through a tap in their hearts, some hear Him through dreams and vision and some people hear Him whispering, regardless what unique way He speaks to you, the primary way God speaks is through His Word the Bible. Or in times of worship.

How you hear is not important but hearing from Him every day is. I want to encourage you with this; God's love for you is so great, and He wants to have an intimate relationship with you, and hearing is a big part of that. Hearing from Him right from the start has been a blessing.

My church family taught me I could hear from God, so on the day that He appeared to me, it was easy to hear Him. Maybe it was instilled in you from a young age that God no longer speaks to His people; this book will dispel that lie once and for all.

Are you ready for the adventure of a lifetime? It is time for you to hear not just from God but learn who He truly is and how he wants to use you to reach a world desperate for His love.

What are you waiting for? Turn the page, and let's start!

Introduction – When Jesus Called My Name

For my father and my mother have forsaken me, but the Lord will take me up.

Psalm 27:10 NASB

I am so thankful for people who hear from the Lord and are willing to be obedient to what He says. They completely changed my life. They were the ones who planted the seeds of Jesus in me and watered them so that when He appeared to me in my room on Jan 3, 1997, I was ready to accept Him.

From the time I was small, Jesus sent Christians into my life to prepare me for that day. I was born into a Muslim family in Nigeria, and they chose me to go to a Muslim school and become an Imam. At the age of two, I became deathly ill. My parents did everything medically they could do for me, but in the end, they could not sit there and watch me die, so they took me out into the forest and left me there to die.

According to what my mother had told me, I was alone for three days, but then my mother came to check on me, found me still alive, and took me home. God had a plan for my life even though the enemy tried to take me out, Jesus protected me.

Around that time, a Christian nurse had come into the area. My parents heard about her and, desperate to try anything to save me, took me to her. She prayed over me both morning and evening each day and night, and I was made well. Jesus had performed a miracle in my life, and that was the start of Him reaching out to me, but it would not be the last.

A Strange Road To Jesus

I did grow up and become a Muslim Imam, and I hated Jesus with everything in me; he was my enemy. At that time, I had moved to Ghana and was in charge of the mosque there, but there was a desire to go back to where I was born and raised, so I went back to Nigeria and decided that was where I wanted to stay.

The first time I went into the mosque there, I had no intention of letting anyone know that I was an Imam, but they found out, and I ended up becoming the Imam there and started another two mosques. Even then, God was preparing me to become a Pastor, Evangelist, Prophet, Teacher, and Apostle.

The funny thing is that I could not stand Jesus, and yet two of my close friends were Christians. It was a love/hate relationship. Who they believed in was my adversary, and yet something about them made me want to be around them?

They would come with their Bibles, and I would have my Koran, and we would argue over which one was the truth. They would get me so upset that I would start to beat them up physically, and all they would say is that they loved me and would come and see me even more. They told me that they were concerned about my soul. I didn't even know what a soul was! It got to the point that I did not want to see them anymore, but they kept coming around.

One particular day they had come and argued, and I just wanted to get rid of them, so I took a pail of water, and I dumped it on their heads and kicked them out. I tried to make it look like they had peed on themselves to embarrass them, but the next day they were back again.

Finally, one day they said, "Zak, we want you to take us to a Christian meeting." I thought about it and said, "If I take you to this Christian meeting, will you leave me alone?" and they said, "Yes." I thought to myself, "Yes, I can get rid of them, finally!"

The meeting was six months away, and I quickly forgot about it. There were no phones in Nigeria at that time to use to remind me of the meeting, so the day came, and they knocked on my door. I told them I could not take them. I had forgotten about it and agreed to take care of a girl paralyzed from the waist down.

They said to me, "Remember the promise you made that you would take us to the stadium if we left you alone? We have no one else to take us, so you have to." I could not back down, so I piled them and the partially crippled girl with her crutches into the car and drove an hour to get there.

Once we got there and parked the car, the Christian guys immediately got out and left. I quickly realized that I had not gotten directions on how to get home, so I got out and started looking for them.

In Nigeria, parking lots do not have lines determining parking spaces, so after I had gotten out, people parked all around me and blocked me in at the back of the stadium. That is when things got interesting...

The Name Of Jesus

I was desperate to get out of there. I kept hiding my face because I was a well-known Imam in that locality, and here I was at a Christian meeting. Some speakers projected everything that was being said outside, and all I kept hearing was, "Jesus! Jesus."

Everything in me wanted to get out of there, but I was stuck. It was hot that day, and the partially crippled girl was getting cranky in the car, so I got her out. There was a bench not far away, and I wanted to get there quickly to continue to hide who I was.

The girl was moving slowly, and I hurried her along when one of her crutches broke and then the other. Now, I had to carry her. At the time I did not know who was preaching, but I found out later that it was Benson Idahosa (a friend of Benny Hinn's).

I could not make out what he was saying, but he kept yelling the name of Jesus. Suddenly, I heard a pop and the girl's one leg started moving, and I was thinking to myself, "What kind of witchcraft and voodoo is this?" I wanted to run as fast as I could. I had never seen someone who was partially paralyzed suddenly move.

I started walking faster to get to the bench, and I heard another pop, and now the girl's other leg was moving too. She kept saying, "I want to walk. I want to walk. Put me down." I said, "If you could walk, then I would not have to carry you." She was persistent, and I would not put her down, so she bit me. I still have the scar to this day. I dropped her to the ground, and right before my very eyes, she got up and walked.

My first thought was, "Who is this Jesus who could touch this girl and heal her? I have known her for a long time, and I know that she is partially paralyzed from her waist down to her feet. Just the name of Jesus alone touched this little girl." Now, I have a problem. I am a Muslim Imam, and Jesus healed this girl in front of my eyes. I can tell you that the hour-long drive home felt like ten hours, and I did not want to go because I was unsure what would happen when I got there.

I made it home safely, and things seemed to be normal. When the girl's parents came home, I told them what had happened, and her mother passed out.

That night I went back to the mosque to do my duties, which included leading prayers in the evening called "Magreb" prayers. I was right in the middle of reciting the prayers when, instead me of saying "Allahu Akbar Allahu Akbar Ashhadu Alla ilaha lllallah, Ashhadu an na Muhammada Rasudanal Allahu Akbar," I said, "Jesus Christ of Nazareth." What I said was heard throughout the mosque and even outside because of the loudspeakers, and everyone knew it was me.

Now, I was in severe trouble, and people wanted to kill me. Thankfully, Jesus protected me and opened up a door for me to come to Canada as a student. I was now in the land of freedom, but I was not happy.

I no longer held the Muslim beliefs, and the name of Jesus got me into trouble, so I became a Pagan. I had a job, and l lived a normal life. It was challenging and hard not having family around. As an African from Ghana, I needed people around me, but because I was rejected and disowned, there was no hope and nothing to live for; I wanted to kill myself and was prepared to do so at 3 am that night.

At that time, there was a knock at my door, and I was upset that someone was knocking at my door at that hour. In Ghana, Africa, people do not usually call; they just show up at your door, but now in Canada, people should call! That was why I was upset, but I proceeded to the door, opened it and looked around, but there was no one there, so I went back to the bedroom, and there was a second knock at the door!

Now I was getting really upset and angry at whoever was knocking at my door at 3 am. So, this time, I pretended I was going to my bedroom by thumping my foot on the floor and waited. This time the knock was much louder, and I opened the door, and I heard this audible, distinct voice and it said, "If your mother and father forsake you, I will be there for you."

Then the voice spoke to me again. "I did not say to the seed of Jacob to seek me in vain." (Isaiah 45:19). Then I said. "Who are you?" And He said, "I am Jesus. I am here to help you."

At that moment, I felt so dirty and yucky, and I was on my knees, crying. He said, "I forgive you. You are the very reason why I died on the cross, and I am here to use you to change lives." I responded, "I am not good enough! I was the one who hated you!" He said, "I love you so much!" and He took his hand and wiped me clean, and then he said, "Now obey my commandments!" Right there, I gave my life to Jesus.

Jesus Wants You

My life has completely changed since I let Jesus in. After that, there was a peace and love that I had never known, and even though my family abandoned me, God never has. Was it always easy? No. Like you, I have my share of struggles, but the difference is now I do not have to go through them alone. The Creator of the Universe is with me, guiding me each step of the way.

I wrote this book because I want you to have the same relationship with Jesus that I do. It is one where you hear His voice and feel His love every day. When you know Him intimately, He shows you each step, protects you from many things, and gives you the honour of bringing Him to others.

In this book, we are going to explore several main themes.

The first one is how to develop a close personal relationship with God. Without that relationship, you have nothing. If you want to walk in the power of God, it must come from a place of intimacy and hearing from Him. When you use God's power without it, it becomes a snare that leads you to a dark place. We will explore what that relationship looks like and how you develop it.

Second, we will look at how to hear from God for others. God does not want you to keep Him all to yourself. He wants you to share what you have learned with others. He also wants you to be able to walk in His power to heal this broken world.

Who Is This Book For?

If you are hungry for God and want Him to move in your life, this book is for you. God wants a bride that will put Him first and the world second. He is looking for those who will be obedient and do what He says.

If you are hoping to read this book to get some hints and tips on using God's power without recognizing that He is God and His ways are not our ways, then this book is not for you. This book teaches you how to hear from God for your life and then follow what He says. God is Sovereign, the ultimate King, and you need to treat Him as such, not to use Him as a sugar daddy.

If you are serious about God and Him moving in your life, then I have a promise for you. This book will help you get there. I will share with you all that I have learned over more than twenty years of walking with Jesus, including the ups and the downs. None of us is perfect, we all make mistakes, but it is how you let God heal those mistakes that make the difference. Are you ready to join me on a journey of discovery? If you are, fasten your seat belts because you are in for the adventure of a lifetime.

Chapter 1: Why Does God Want To Speak With Us?

We love, because He first loved us.

1 John 4:19 NASB

"God, is that you?" Katelyn whispered. All of a sudden, love and warmth filled her heart. She had never experienced this before. Tears of joy and healing started to roll down her cheek. She could hardly believe it was real, yet she could not deny what was happening.

For the last few years, Katelyn had struggled. She had given her life to Jesus, and yet not much on the inside had changed. Outwardly, she had given up many things in the world. Katelyn read the Word, went to church, Bible studies, and prayer meetings regularly. She was learning more about Him through the Bible, but the more she read, the more her heart yearned for more. Katelyn wanted to experience God the way many in the Word had-personally. She longed to have God speak to her and direct her life.

She recently moved into a new area and decided to try a different church. She had heard about the Holy Spirit and wanted to learn more about Him. The church she had attended before did not teach on that subject, but she knew that there had to be more. Her heart was hungry for something, but she did not know what it was.

This new church had told her that God wanted to have a personal relationship with her. Jesus, through the Holy Spirit, wanted to fill her to overflowing with His presence and love, and she asked God to give her more of Him.

Nothing seemed to happen at the church, but later, when Katelyn was sitting at home on her couch listening to worship music, she started to feel something she had never felt before, a love that was beyond words. At that moment, she knew that Jesus LOVED HER with an unconditional love. All she could say was, "Thank you."

A few moments later, it started to change, and she could hear Jesus speaking to her. It was a blend of words and impressions in her mind. He was telling her that tomorrow when she went to work, she needed to say to a fellow employee that it would be okay, and that God was with Him.

What she had longed for was occurring. God wanted to use her to reach the world…

His Love Is So Great

The first reason why God wants to speak to us is He loves us, pure and simple. The Creator of the whole universe handcrafted you with love. It is a love so powerful that even hell itself cannot conquer it, and it must be communicated.

Everything God does is because of His love. The only reason we came to know Him was because He reached out in love to us first. It was His love that drew us in and taught us to love. Ephesians 1:4-6 NASB says,

> *Just as He chose us in Him before the foundation of the world, that we would be holy and blameless before Him. In love, He predestined us to adoption as sons through Jesus Christ to Himself, according to the kind intention of His will, to the praise of the glory of His grace, which He freely bestowed on us in the Beloved.*

You did not come to God first. He reached out to you, and you responded. Sin keeps us separated from God, and like Adam and Eve in the garden, we hide from Jesus. But His love is so great that He comes and calls out our name and invites us to become His loved ones.

The love of God is so immense that there is nowhere you can go to be separated from it. God is love, and His love is perfect, and He loves you perfectly the way you are. He loves you whether you love Him back or not.

God's love is so powerful that even an ex-Muslim such as I, who hated Him with everything within me, could not help but be drawn to the love He gave me. His love melted my heart.

Let us be clear about one thing. God does not need your love. He is complete within Himself. Your love does not change who God is. He wants and desires your love, and that is why He paid such a high price to get it.

When Adam and Eve sinned, it created a gulf between God and man. God is perfect and sinless, and sin cannot be in His presence. Sin must be paid for by someone sinless. Since none of us is sinless, God sent His son Jesus to pay the price for us.

Jesus came to earth as a man, lived a sinless life, and then sacrificed Himself on the Cross to pay for every sin we have ever and will ever commit. It cost Him everything so we could have fellowship with Him. He loves us so much. He was willing to do that on our behalf.

It is a gift that God offers us, and if we accept it and ask Jesus into our hearts, He will forgive us, and we will have a relationship with Him, here on this earth and go to Heaven when we die. There is nothing you can do to earn His love; you can only accept it.

If you have never asked Jesus to forgive your sins and come into your heart, go to www.gariba.org or zkgariba@yahoo.ca or zak@gariba.org and send me a message. I would love to lead you to Jesus.

He Desires Relationship With Us

The second reason God speaks to us is He wants to have a relationship with us, and one of the core foundations of any relationship is communication.

There are two different aspects of the relationship. God loves us, and we fall in love with Him. A human relationship is two different people who have something in common and are attracted to one another. As they get to know each other, the bond between them grows and becomes love, whether it is love for family members, romantic love, or friendship love.

15

God is different, and we must always remember that. Jesus desires a deep, intimate relationship with us, but it is never equal. After all, He is God. Jesus' love never changes for us. It is complete the way it is. He already paid the ultimate price for His love; Jesus died for us. He showed us the extent of what He was willing to go through for us to be connected to Him. I am writing this just before Easter, and I think about just how much His love cost Him.

It is our love for Him that grows, and as we draw closer to Him, He reveals himself more to us, and the relationship grows stronger. As we do, God also starts to speak to our hearts because He knows us completely well. There is nothing that is a surprise to Him. He knows every thought and feeling. He even has every hair on your head numbered, (Luke 12:7) including me who has a few hairs left on my head. Smile!

When we are first saved, Jesus speaks to us through His Word as we read it, or listen to sermons and Bible studies, and that is good. The Bible is God's Word, and we need to read it daily, learn it, and memorize it. It shows us how to live a godly life. If the Bible says one thing and someone teaches you something else, go with what the Bible says.

That is not the only way God speaks to us. He wants an intimate relationship where He can talk directly to us about our lives and the lives of others.

He wants to protect us from danger, heal our hearts, and help us reach out to the dying world.

Many denominations and Preachers teach that the only way to hear from God is through His word, which is not true. Throughout the Bible in both the Old and New Testament, God spoke to people personally, and since God does not change, He still speaks to us today. He wants to be involved in our lives. Let me share a story with you about my friend Kim. When she accepted Jesus, she learned that you only hear from God through the Word.

After her baptism with the Holy Spirit, a year later, she began a journey of learning to hear God personally for her life. She told me about the first time she heard God speak to her:

I had been asking God to speak to me, and I was practicing listening to His voice, but nothing seemed to be happening.

A couple that we had not seen in a long time had come to visit, and my husband was fixing our friend's stereo. He needed batteries for his meter, and since I was driving into town (half an hour away) to get a few things, I said I would pick some up. The wife came with me, so we could have a chance to chat.

When we got to the store, I went to the battery section, picked up a package of batteries and put it in my basket, and started to walk away. I immediately had the thought, "Kim, don't you think you should call your husband and make sure you got the right batteries?" I quickly dismissed the idea because I knew that I had the right ones.

The same thought came to me two more times, each time stronger than the other. I stopped in the middle of the store and said to my friend, "I think God is trying to tell me that I bought the wrong batteries." She looked at me strangely, but I decided to call my husband and guess what? I had the wrong ones.

I was embarrassed that I had remembered the wrong ones, but there was also this joy in my heart as I realized that God had answered my prayer, and I could hear His voice. Since then, I hear God regularly in many different ways. Each time He speaks, I still get that same sense of awe that the God of the Universe would care enough about me to help me.

To Equip Us

God also speaks to us to equip us to reach a lost and dying world. He tells us things to say to others and gives us gifts that we can use to show His love to the world. Later in this book, there is a whole chapter on His giftings; what they are, and how you use them. God calls us to share his love, not be selfish, and hoard it. Jesus wants us full and overflowing so that we have more than enough to share with others.

The love of God is so big that it includes all of the earth and each person in it. When we have a relationship with Him, He starts to speak to us about how we can reach those who need Him.

I had an experience not too long ago, where I led a church service, and I saw a picture of my ex-girlfriend whose last name we will call Brown. I looked around the church, but I did not see anyone that looked like her and was relieved. It disturbed me a bit because I was standing beside my wife Karen-Marie that the Lord had given me, but I felt Him impress upon my heart that He wanted me to share what I had seen. So, I did.

After the service, a woman came up to me and told me that her last name is Brown, the same as my ex-girlfriend's last name. She started to cry, and it was apparent that the Lord was all over her. I ministered to her, and Karen-Marie led her in a sinner's prayer, and she gave her life to Jesus.

As you walk with Him, He will start to speak to you not only about your life but about others as well.

Intimacy And Prophecy

There are two sections in this book: Intimacy and Prophecy. The Intimacy section is about you and your relationship with the Lord. It is the foundation for everything else. Without that relationship, you will not be able to hear His voice for others effectively. Then in the Prophecy section, you will learn about hearing God for your own life and others. You will also learn about His other gifts and their use in your life.

Just before we end this chapter, I want to share one more thing with you: hope. When I first came to know the Lord, I was a mess. My heart was broken, and my life was in shambles. I had tried to commit suicide because of the rejection I felt.

In Africa, being a part of the community was everything. When I said the name Jesus in the Mosque, everything tore away from me. Both my family and my community not only rejected me but wanted to kill me. When I came to Canada, I felt alone, angry, and unlovable, and I tried to end it all. Thankfully, God had other plans for my life.

After I came to know Jesus, He started to heal those broken places as I drew near Him. Now, I know that I am loved completely, even if no one else ever loves me, the Lord does. As my life started to change, He began to speak to me about others.

If you are in a place of brokenness right now, the Lord wants to heal your heart.

In the name of Jesus, I pray that the Holy Spirit will touch you and heal your heart from whenever you may have been abused; physically, emotionally, mentally, sexually or financially. God is healing you right now. He is healing you of rejection, abandonment, fears, etc. I pray God will take away all these yucky feelings and replace them with His love.

I also pray that you may encounter the living Jesus. May He be intimate with you. May you draw closer as He draws closer to you.

I encourage you to grow in intimacy in your relationship with the Lord by reading the Word, spending time with Him and getting to know who He is. As you do your life can change.

If the Lord can use someone like me who was who was homeless, imagine what He can do in you!

You can't rely on the world's system. Rely on God's Kingdom.

Pastor Zak

Chapter 2: Intimacy Is the Only Way to Hear God

The Lord appeared to him from afar, saying,
"I have loved you with an everlasting love;
Therefore I have drawn you
with lovingkindness.

Jeremiah 31:3 NASB

I never knew what true love and intimacy were until I met Jesus. Like most, I thought I knew what they were, but as I got to know Him, I realized how pale it was in comparison to what Jesus felt for me.

Love your God with all your heart, might and soul and love your neighbour as yourself. How can you love your neighbour when you cannot love yourself, Intimacy is loving yourself? Learning to love yourself would change your life as well.

Unconditional love is neutral and has no opposite polarity. The source of unconditional love is Holy Spirit; therefore, it is available to everyone and there is absolutely nothing we need to do to qualify for it. Unconditional love comes through to us at a soul level, beginning at the level of self-acceptance and self-forgiveness, and radiates divine light to everyone and everything.

When we make a conscious decision to choose thoughts based on unconditional love, it does not mean that we agree with everyone and everything. It means that we consciously commit ourselves to express respect, kindness, and cooperation to everyone and everything in our environment.

Unconditional love is not something that happens to us or outside of us. It is the life force of energy within our very being and is ingrained in every cell of our bodies. We do not have to search for love–we ARE, each of us, the physical embodiment of unconditional love. Because unconditional love is life energy, it is formless, infinite, always in motion, and unconditionally available to us 24/7!

It changed my life!

What is Intimacy? To me, it means four things:

1. Having a close relationship with someone.

2. A way of expressing love to someone in a way that they can understand.

3. The desire to fall in love with somebody.

4. Loving someone whether they can reciprocate it back to you. For example, a mother loves her baby and young child even though that child cannot show it.

All of these describe how God loves us. One of the things that amaze me is that God wants and desires to have a close, personal, deep bond with me, someone who hated Him and would gladly have put Him on the cross myself. It humbles me, and all I can do is be grateful and accept it.

As I thought about this word, another way of saying the word came to me.

Into-Me-See

That is what we will talk about in this chapter, how God sees into us and how He lets us see into Him. You will be astonished at how your life changes once you get to know the God of the Universe.

The Best Earthly Example Of Intimacy

There is one earthy relationship that is closest to the relationship we have with the Lord, and that is a marriage between a husband and a wife. Two people who met fell in love and chose to spend the rest of their life together. The two become one.

Everyone who is saved is also the Bride of Christ, and one day we will join Him in the marriage supper of the Lamb. In 2 Corinthians 11:2 NASB, Paul writes,

> *For I am jealous for you with a godly jealousy; for I betrothed you to one husband, so that to Christ I might present you as a pure virgin.*

That is how Jesus loves us, with that close intimate love. Many characteristics of a good marriage also apply to our relationship with Jesus. Let's take a look at them.

Trust

When I became a Christian, I needed assurance that everything would be okay, and He gave me that. I started to trust Him and bring my walls down. When I did that, I got to know Him more and could trust Him for more.

It is like when you are first married and still getting to comprehend how much that other person loves you. As you test that love, you come to the point that you know you can trust your spouse with everything you are. It is built over years of it being proven.

The same is with God. As we get to know Him, we can trust Him for more and more. As we give God opportunities to prove that He is trustworthy, our belief becomes secure. Even during the most challenging times, we know that Jesus is taking care of us.

Vulnerability

For us, humans, I think vulnerability is one of the most challenging aspects of our relationship with Him. It started in the garden when Adam and Eve hid from God because of their sin. We do not want to open ourselves up because we are afraid of what we think God will see.

What we do not realize is that God knows us better than we know ourselves. We cannot hide anything from Him. Before time even began, He saw our entire life, including every action and every thought.

Not only does God know us intimately, but He also loves us, just as we are. Every time I think of that, my heart floods with emotion and appreciation of how wonderful Jesus is.

I want to encourage you to open your heart to Him today. If there is something that you have been holding back, it is time to let it go. I feel the Lord saying, "Open up your heart just a little. Take that step of faith and let Me show you that I am trustworthy. I know that your situation is difficult. Right now, you feel like you might not make it through, but I AM faithful. I AM everything you need. Do not give up. I will bring you through that valley into a beautiful place."

Communication

I have heard stories of women who are unhappy in their marriage because their husbands do not tell them that they love them. Their attitude is, "I married you. I told you I loved you on our wedding day, and we are still married. Why do I need to keep telling you," Those relationships are heading for divorce?

One of the best ways to have a healthy marriage is to communicate honestly with each other. You need to talk, talk, talk and talk some more and then be willing to listen with an open heart. As the relationship grows, you will share your emotions in a kind and loving way.

It is same with God. You need daily communion with Him. You need to tell Him how much you love Him and then listen as He expresses the same back to you.

Forgiveness

Forgiveness is one of the most powerful tools in marriage. We are human, and we make mistake.

We do not understand each other, and we hurt each other. Forgiveness allows us to let go of the past and live in the present, keeping the relationship strong.

We also need to keep short accounts with God. Sin separates us from Him, and the longer we go without asking His forgiveness, the further we pull away from Him. Eventually, if we do not humble ourselves before God, we will have taken ourselves out of his grace completely.

Forgiveness cleans us and allows us to live a life of freedom, open to His presence and voice.

Intimacy Is Essential To Hearing From God

This world system tells us to use our natural minds to make decisions. The education system never has us use our spirits to hear from God. We have been taught to be independent and choose what we want.

Our natural state is a selfish one. Your mind and your flesh do not want to hear from God. It fights what God wants. That is why intimacy is vital.

When we draw near to God, we acknowledge that we cannot do this on our own. We see that we have failings and that we do not know everything. When we come close to Him, it allows us to humble ourselves, and when we do, we can hear His voice for our lives.

Jesus is omniscient, meaning He knows everything and what is best for you. His desire is for you to live a life that brings honour and glory to Him. When we do that, life becomes wonderful. It does not mean that we do not go through difficult things. There are times when life is hard, but when we are close to Jesus, it is like being in the eye of the storm. It may swirl around us, but it does not destroy us. We can have peace and even joy during troubles.

God wants to share with you things that will not only help you but protect you at the same time There have been many times I have gone to do something, and I heard God's warning and realized that would not have been good for me.

A friend of mine experience's food allergies, especially to a particular preservative. There are many foods you would not think of that have this-preservative. She has learned to trust God, and there have been many times that He has cautioned her about a product and when she looked at the ingredients, sure enough, it was there. Even commonplace things like certain kinds of vinegar contain it. Now, when she hears that whisper, she listens to it, knowing that God is protecting her from harm.

God wants to be a part of your life. He wants to guide you. In Isaiah 30:21 NASB, God says,

> *Your ears will hear a word behind you,*
> *"This is the way, walk in it," whenever*
> *you turn to the right or to the left.*

There is a cost to hearing God like that, and it is intimacy with Him. Think of it this way. With whom do you share your most intimate inner thoughts?

Here is the amazing thing about God. He does not require a certain level of closeness before He speaks to you. He is not stingy with His love and wisdom. He shares it freely and wants you to know it. The problem is on our end. Our minds and our flesh cannot hear God. They are worldly and fight Him until we learn to control them. It is our spirit that hears from God. That is why we need to spend time in prayer and worship, to allow our spirit time to connect with God.

God Is Not A Sugar Daddy

Have you ever been somewhere, and you saw this beautiful young woman on the arm of a much older man and thought to yourself, "She's only with him because of his money?" That is what a sugar daddy is. He gives her whatever she wants, and she pretends to love him.

Jesus is not like that at all, and we should never treat Him that way. Many Christians and non-Christians alike base their love for God on what He will give them. If he does not provide them with something, they do not love Him.

A lot of Christians struggle with this because they need God to give them something, answer their prayer or heal them. They do not go to Him first because they love Him; they go to Him to get something.

If you are reading this and feel a nudge from the Holy Spirit, I want you to repent of that attitude and ask God to forgive you and restore a right relationship with Him. We are human, and sometimes our flesh gets in the way. The best thing to do is to recognize it and deal with it.

Intimacy solves this issue. As you fall in love with Him, you stop seeking His hands for what He can give you, and you start looking at His face in worship.

When you are close to the Lord, two things occur – trust and faith. You trust that He loves you and has your best interests at heart. It is a deep knowing inside of you that your life in His hands, and that is an excellent place to be.

Trust is hard, especially when people have let you down when you needed them the most, or instead of loving you, they have hurt or abused you. But God is not like that. He is completely trustworthy because He is perfect and His love towards you is perfect. He is also a patient parent and gives you lots of opportunities to learn to trust Him more.

If you are a parent, think of when your child was learning to stand and walk. You did not get mad because they stood and fell, then stood, took a half step and decided to crawl. You cheered them on and encouraged them to take that next step. God is the same; every time you try, He opens His arms even wider and invites you to come to Him.

Faith

The Bible says,

> *Now faith is the assurance of things hoped for, the conviction of things not seen.*
> *Hebrews 11:1 NASB*

Faith is knowing beyond a shadow of a doubt that God will give you what you need when you need it. That can be frustrating because we think we know what we need and when we need it. Many times, those needs are wants that are not good for us or they are needed but the timing has to be right because we are not ready for it.

For example – Lots of people who win the lottery are broke within five years. Why? They did not have the skills to handle that amount of wealth and spent it foolishly. What should have lasted them a lifetime was gone in a few short years with nothing to show for it.

Faith allows us to believe God for big things and trust that it will come in the right timing but in the meantime, our needs will be met.

How To Experience Intimacy With God?

Intimacy with God is the most incredible thing you will experience in life. I wish I could tell you exactly how to get there but we are all individuals with unique hearts but I can give you a starting place and that is prayer, worship and reading His Word. In my experience, you will find that place of intimacy in one of those three areas.

The most important thing is this; spend time with Him daily and intentionally open your heart to receive from Him what He has for you. You may experience Him differently from me, but I guarantee that you when you do it will be powerful.

In the next chapter we will look at why people lose their first love and how that impacts your effectiveness in God.

Chapter 3: Why Christians Lose Their First Love

But I have this against you, that you have left your first love. Therefore, remember from where you have fallen, and repent and do the deeds you did at first; or else I am coming to you and will remove your lampstand out of its place—unless you repent. Revelation 2:4-5

I remember a young man named John (not his real name) who got saved and was on fire for the Lord. The joy he exuded was infectious. He loved Jesus with his whole heart, and he spent his time telling people about God, and he was happy. Every time I saw him, I was encouraged. Regularly, he was bringing people to the Lord, and I saw him grow as a Christian. In our church, he was becoming a respected Evangelist, and I saw leadership potential in him.

35

Then things started to change. John's girlfriend was not happy with him and broke up with him. He did not deal with it well. Instead of turning to the Lord and allowing Him to heal his heart, he started to pull away. He stopped sharing about Jesus and eventually did not come to church anymore.

The sad part is instead of leaning into God; he started to listen to others who told him what his broken heart wanted to hear. They shared how they had 'tried' God, and He let them down. The last time I saw him, the happiness was gone, and I found out later that all he does is isolate himself in his room and play video games on the internet.

How did this vibrant young man fall so far below his potential? He lost his first love.

What Is Your First Love?

When we become a born-again Christian, God impacts His love upon us, and that is why we can love Him back. That love fills our hearts, and we start to read His Word, worship and pray.

That first love often is intense, like the first time you 'fell in love' as a teenager. It is strong, and the only thing you can think about is God. It overwhelms you, and you want to do everything possible to please the Lord. It is an amazingly wonderful time as you get to know Him.

When I first met Jesus, all I wanted to do was to be near Him. I desired intimacy. I had never experienced that before in my life, and each encounter with God made me hunger for more.

Was your experience like that? Maybe yours was a quieter one. Some people are more logical than emotional. Possibly your first love resulted in hunger for His Word and learning about Him?

Everyone experiences God in their own way, but when you first come to Jesus, and He starts changing your life, that is called your first love. It is the honeymoon period from your perspective in your relationship with Him.

It is a crucial stage as it creates the foundation for the rest of your Christian walk. If your foundation is strong, you will serve the Lord passionately for the rest of your life. If it is not, then there is a chance that you will lose your first love and fall away from God, or it may go stagnant and be unfruitful.

Why People Lose Their First Love

In Matthew 13: 3-8 NASB, Jesus told a story:

*And He spoke many things to them
in parables, saying, "Behold, the sower went
out to sow; and as he sowed, some seeds fell
beside the road, and the birds came and ate
them up. Others fell on the rocky places,
where they did not have much soil; and
immediately they sprang up, because they*

*had no depth of soil. But when the sun had
risen, they were scorched; and because they
had no root, they withered away. Others
fell among the thorns, and the thorns came
up and choked them out. And others fell on
the good soil and yielded a crop, some
a hundredfold, some sixty, and some thirty.*

I believe that God provides an additional layer of protection and love when you are first saved. It is like a newborn. As a parent, you have special equipment like cribs, car seats, playpens, hats and clothing all designed to protect your precious child. God is the same way. He gives you the time you need to get to know Him a bit, but things will happen to test that love. Like we talked about in the last chapter, God is not a sugar daddy, and your love for Him has to grow beyond what God can give you.

Three things that can happen when you are first saved:

1. You continue to grow stronger in the Lord.

2. You fade away because you have no root.

3. Something happens that makes you question your trust in God.

Hopefully, because you are reading this book and the Bible, you are an example of number one as mentioned above, but you need to be aware of the other two.

38

Sometimes when someone comes to know the Lord, they are all excited and by outward appearances are doing great, but on the inside, they are not developing that close, intimate relationship with Him. The reasons for not developing the relationship can be abuse, mental health issues; their flesh is strong and has control, or the people around them are discouraging them.

Whatever the case is, they become a flash in the pan. Here one day and gone the next. They join because of the excitement of it, but they cannot commit to making it work. Some want a sense of family and belonging but do not want to give control to anyone else. For others, they did because someone else did, and they did not want to let the other person down.

Either way, God has not taken root in their life. He has not become real, and therefore it is easy to leave. It would be hard to say if they ever had a first love to begin with, but some may have.

The third point listed above, "Questioning your trust in God", I find the most discouraging.

As it was with John, some start strong and seem to be doing well with the Lord. They come to church and participate. They are reading the Word, praying and worshiping. Then, something happens that makes them question their faith in God. That is God's love and trust test. Can you continue to love

Him and draw close to Him even when things do not go the way you want?

At some point in your relationship with God, you will hit this point, and it is what you do in this time that determines your future. The Lord will allow tribulations in your walk to test your faith and love. That is how it grows, but the first time it happens can be one of the hardest.

It is hard when the world, the flesh, and the devil pull you away from the Lord. The world is the people in it that do not belong to Jesus and the systems that govern it. They tell you that you are crazy to serve God. God is not real, why can you not go out and have some fun. Sometimes they will even persecute you for knowing Jesus. My family did.

The flesh is the ungodly desires and lusts that you have in your life. When you are first saved, it is your flesh that controls most things; as you grow in the Lord, you learn how to give Him control.

Satan's goal is to see you pulled away from Jesus. The devil will send demons to speak to your mind and tell you that, "you cannot trust God or that there are greener pastures over there. Life is boring when you serve God. He is a killjoy; you know better than He does". These are lies whispered in your ear in hopes that you will listen and consider it. When you do ponder the lies, that is when you start to lose that first love.

Sometimes It Quietly Fades Away

The most significant time of temptation to lose your first love is when you are coming out of the honeymoon period, but it is not the only time. In Revelations 3:15-19 NASB it says:

> *'I know your deeds, that you are neither cold nor hot; I wish that you were cold or hot. So, because you are lukewarm, and neither hot nor cold, I will spit you out of My mouth. Because you say, "I am rich, and have become wealthy, and have need of nothing," and you do not know that you are wretched and miserable and poor and blind and naked, I advise you to buy from Me gold refined by fire so that you may become rich, and white garments so that you may clothe yourself, and that the shame of your nakedness will not be revealed; and eye salve to anoint your eyes so that you may see. Those whom I love, I reprove and discipline; therefore, be zealous and repent.*

Those words from the Lord are incredibly strong. It shows that over time if you are not intentionally spending time with the Lord that your love can fade away. You become too comfortable, and life is too good. You do not need anything from God. When that happens, that is when you reach the danger zone. If you don't turn back, you will become lukewarm. I regularly pray that I never become lukewarm, so that the Lord wants to spit me out of His mouth.

What To Do If Your First Love Has Faded Away?

First of all, there is one crucial thing to understand. God has never stopped loving you. He has and will always be head-over-heels in love with you, and He still shows you love each day. God has never moved away from you. It is you who have moved away from Him.

I have heard people say that God does not love them anymore, and that is why they do not love Him. That is not true. God's love is everlasting; you are never without it. There is nothing that you can do to stop Him from loving you.

What happens is as you start to move away from God, you see, hear and feel Him less and less. You do not read His word as much, and your prayer life fades so you are not reminded of Jesus. Then you stop having fellowship with other Christians. You give yourself excuses for doing it, but ultimately you are the one who suffers for it.

There is only one way to come to the Lord, and that is – REPENTANCE.

In 1 John 1:9 NASB, God says:

> *If we confess our sins, He is faithful and righteous to forgive us our sins and to cleanse us from all unrighteousness.*

What is repentance? It is recognizing that we have done wrong and turning our hearts back to Him. You come before Him and tell Him, "God, I made a mistake, I have fallen out of love with You. I have stopped trusting You and praying to you and reading Your Word. Would you forgive me?" When you do that, God is faithful and just and will not only forgive you but cleanses you. He gives you a clean slate.

Once you have accepted His incredible forgiveness, do not turn back to those wicked ways. Start fresh. Ask Jesus to give you the grace and the strength not to go back but to go forward with Him. In God's eyes, those sins are gone, and He remembers them no more.

You may be wondering how God can forget your sin if He knows everything from the moment that time began? God does not forget, but He chooses not to bring it to His remembrance. When the Lord looks at you, He does not see the sin. He sees you with eyes of love.

That is the way you need to look at yourself. Do not let in guilt and shame. In Romans 8:1 NASB, Paul writes:

> *Therefore, there is now no condemnation for those who are in Christ Jesus.*

Now that the sin is gone, it is time for you to renew the intimacy with Him. Ask the Holy Spirit to teach you not to lose that first love again. Ask Him for hunger for His Word, prayer and worship again. God loves that kind of prayer and will do as you ask. Many times, that second love is even more amazing than the first.

I want to encourage you. No matter where you are at with the Lord, there is more of Him to experience. Please pray this with me:

Lord give me a hunger for your Word: give me a hunger for souls, and a hunger to search for the hidden things of God, so I can know your will for my life. May I always yield to the will of God. Amen.

Hunger and faith bring you closer to God. If you prayed that prayer with an honest heart, get ready. God is about to move mightily in your life.

In the next chapter, we will talk more about the obstacles that can try to come into your life to take away your intimacy with God. Study this chapter carefully as it will keep you, *"Strong in the Lord and in the strength of His might." Ephesians 6:10 NASB*

Chapter 4: The 8 Blockages to Intimacy with God

*Now Saul was afraid of David, for
the LORD was with him but had departed
from Saul. Therefore, Saul removed him
from his presence and appointed him as his
commander of a thousand; and he went out
and came in before the people. David was
prospering in all his ways
for the LORD was with him.*

1 Samuel 18:12-14 NASB

Most people know that King David was the Bible's most famous king who brought peace to Israel for many years. But did you know that he was not Israel's first king? Saul was! He lost the kingdom, and it was given to David for one reason - David had intimacy with God and Saul did not.

Saul played around with God. On the outside, he was strong and handsome, and everyone admired Saul. By the world's standards, he was a fantastic choice. Israel cried out for a King, and God gave them the one that they wanted. In the background, God was preparing the one that He wanted to be king, David.

Saul told people he was God's man, but David lived it. The real test was how they dealt with sin. When Saul sinned, he made excuses and did not repent. When David did wrong, he came before the Lord humbly and repented sincerely. David turned to the Lord while Saul turned away. Ultimately, Saul lost what had been given to him, and his entire family as well. Whereas David's family still lives to this day, many generations later, and especially in Jesus. Intimacy is what keeps us close to God and in His will for our lives.

The World, The Flesh And The Devil

In John 6:63 NASB it says,

> *It is the Spirit who gives life; the flesh profits nothing; the words that I have spoken to you are spirit and are life.*

It is sad to say, but even as Christians, we are not taught to live by the Spirit. We often allow our flesh to rule and do whatever it tells us to do. Our flesh is our physical body and its desires. From the time we are born, we were told that our body reigns and is in control. Our flesh is not in submission to God. The flesh is selfish and wants what it wants, no matter the consequences.

As a born-again Christian, it is our responsibility to learn to allow the Spirit to rule what we feed into our life. When we fill ourselves with the Spirit, then the Spirit rules.

The world is all the systems and mindsets that go against God. What the world sees as good is usually evil, and the things that God calls pure and holy the world calls outdated, old-fashioned and outright wrong.

One of the things that the world says is, "Act on what YOU feel is right and good," and as long as it is popular in the world right now, it will be supported. If you act on what the Bible says is good and right, the world will not accept it. It is hypocrisy, and yet the world is blinded to it.

Jesus never did what the world of His time told Him to do. He always did what His Father told Him to do.

Therefore, Jesus answered and was saying to them, "Truly, truly, I say to you, the Son can do nothing of Himself, unless it is something, He sees the Father doing; for whatever the Father does, these things the Son also does in like manner.

John 5:19 NASB

The devil is God's enemy and hates Him with everything in him. It is the goal of Satan and his demons to draw you away from God. They speak lies to your mind to confuse you, and do things to entice your flesh to want to rule and use the world to try to conform you to its image.

Have you ever tried to do something for God, and it seems like everything has come against you to keep you from doing it? That's because everything IS coming against you. Satan is the enemy, and he hates you because you love Jesus, and he wants to derail you from accomplishing your God-given purpose and will use whatever he can to do it.

The devil knows your weaknesses and will use them against you. He cannot read your mind but has studied humanity so much it does not take long to figure out what makes you tick. He will whisper things to you to make you doubt. He will show you things that tempt your flesh and manipulate those around you to convince you that serving Jesus is the wrong thing to do.

Thankfully, when the Spirit leads us, we can overcome all those things.

The 8 Blockages To Following God

Knowledge is power and wisdom is how you carry it out. When you know what hinders you, you start to have the strength to overcome it. Each of these blockages falls under one of the three categories, the world, the flesh and the devil. As you read through them, pray and ask God to show where your blockages are. Once you know that, you can fight it with the Holy Spirit's help.

Not Crucifying The Flesh

All of your life, your flesh has ruled and controlled you. You learned to obey it's desires and wants, and you accepted it as normal. The flesh is selfish. When you are angry, your flesh screams at you to retaliate, and you do. You lust after things that are not good for you, and give in. Your heart gets emotional, and you betray those closest to you.

How do you conquer the flesh and its wants? You learn to follow the Spirit. 1 Corinthians 15:31 NASB it says,

> *I affirm, brethren, by the boasting in you*
> *which I have in Christ Jesus our*
> *Lord, I die daily.*

Every morning when I wake up, I pray to the Lord and ask Him to help me crucify my flesh. Then during the day, as temptations arise, I pray and ask God to take them away from me.

It is a process. In the beginning, it was tough to resist the flesh, but as I did, the Lord infused me with strength, and I was able to overcome it. I would tell those desires in me that they had to die and l would continue resisting until they did, some days I have even laid hands on my head and told it to go away, that I live my life for Jesus.

Jesus has given you authority over your own body, and you can command it. You have the choice to give in to your flesh or yield control to God.

Not Picking Up Your Cross

When we pick up our Cross, we are dying to self and the things that are causing us not to follow God. When we put the Cross before us, it creates a visual that allows everything else to fade into the background.

When Jesus went to the Cross, that was the ultimate defeat over the flesh. In the Garden of Gethsemane, Jesus sweat drops of blood as He agonized over going to the Cross. Jesus knew the price that He was to pay, and He chose to do it, even though it cost Him His life. The price He paid gives us the strength to conquer fear, worry, anger, self-doubt, greed, offense and all other temptations.

When you get to know Jesus through the Word of God and prayer, you will get that strength. Then as He starts to speak to your heart, you can choose not to do those things anymore. It is not always easy. Many times, it is a battle. Your flesh will demand its way, like a spoiled child, and you have to learn to say no until it stops. The more you do this, the easier it gets until one day you realize that it is gone and does not tempt you anymore.

Not Being Vulnerable Before God

One of the things that will start happening when we lose our first love is, we stop being vulnerable before the Lord. We stop opening up our hearts to Him and letting Him in. We hide our sins and think we can do things on our own. That is a dangerous place because we start to lose our intimacy with Him.

A friend of mine started to feel like the amazing things he did was on his own. He began to believe the enemy's lies that told him that he did not need God's help. He decided to test it.

Glen is a miracle worker when it comes to fixing machines and electronics, and one day He asked the Lord not to help him fix a problem with a machine at work, and the Lord granted him his request. Glen quickly realized that his wisdom and way with equipment were part of the gifts the Lord gives him. Thankfully, he repented quickly and drew back close to the Lord.

Sometimes, we are afraid of what God will think of us. We feel if we open our hearts to Him, he will reject us. Let me assure you. God will never leave you nor forsake you. His love for you is greater than anything you have done. Draw close to Him and let Him prove His love for you.

Never stop being vulnerable before God. He loves it when we are transparent with Him, and He draws close when we open ourselves up to Him. He shares His secrets with us, the closer we are to Him.

Not Being In Charge

Some people want the blessings that knowing the Lord brings, but do not want to submit control to Him. Once life gets bad, they come crying back to the Lord to fix it, and He does. When things are good, they think that they can take charge. Leaving the Lord, when things are good to run back when things are bad is an unhappy way to live life.

There can only be one head, and Jesus will never be subject to you.

When you choose to be in charge of your life, God sits back like a parent of a stubborn child and says something like, "You think that you know better. Go ahead and do it your way. I will be here when you find out the truth."

The easiest solution is to open your hands and release your life to God, committing everything to Him. Through many years of experience, I have learned that when God is in control, everything goes as it should, and God brings good out of every situation.

There is freedom in not having to be in charge of your own life. When you trust God to direct your life the way that He wants, it becomes an adventure where you know that you cannot lose. It does not mean that everything is easy in life. We live in a fallen world, and sometimes bad things happen, but I can trust that no matter what happens, God is there and will help me through it.

God also protects you from many things when you put Him in charge. One day God said that I should get up from my office and go home NOW. I got up immediately and left. People started to ask me, "Where are you going?" I ignored them and went out the door.

It usually takes me about twelve minutes to get home from my office, but somehow it took me only two minutes to get there! That itself is a miracle. When I got home, I opened my door, and there was so much smoke in the house! When I had left the house to go to the office to prepare to preach the evening service, I was cooking some chicken, and I left it on the stove without turning it off. God saved my house because I obeyed His voice.

You can trust God with your life.

Not Trusting God

Can I admit something to you? Not trusting God is one of the hardest ones for me. From a young age, I trusted the Koran. Then I found out that it was not true). Even though I loved Jesus with my whole heart now, there was a part of me that questioned if I could really trust God or would I find out later that the Bible was false too.

It has been a long journey, but God is so faithful. He would confirm my trust in Him with words of knowledge and wisdom and the Prophetic. As I heard His voice and I saw the things He told me would come true, I was able to trust Him more.

In Amos 3:7 NASB it says,

Surely the Lord God does nothing
Unless He reveals His secret counsel
To His servants the prophets.

As I trusted Him more, He revealed more of Himself to me. He not only told me things about my life, but others' lives as well. Trust is a process and if God has been asking you to trust Him with something, then take that first step, and you will be amazed at what happens when He comes through for you. As your trust grows, you can believe Jesus for bigger and bigger things.

Another thing. Sometimes we can trust God in certain areas of our life and not others. That is normal, and the Holy Spirit is patient. He works with us just as we are.

Fear

It is a big one. Even though I loved Jesus, I was afraid of God the Father. My earthly father was very harsh, and if I did anything wrong, he would be angry with me. For the longest time, I was afraid to go to God with my sins because I equated Him with my dad. I thought that God would be unforgiving and not love me. I expected to hear the same words that my dad spoke over me.

Yet God never did any of those things. When I conquered my fear and came to Him, He was gentle and loving, and never condemned me. God forgave me and filled me with His love, time and time again.

Fear is one of the tools that the enemy uses in our life. He makes us afraid to get close to God for fear that something terrible will happen.

How do we get rid of fear? By conquering it! By doing what you are afraid to do, no matter what your body or mind says. The first time is the hardest.

The more you do it, the less scared you become, and one day that fear is gone.

What People Will Think

I remember the first time I prophesied over someone. The Pastor of my church asked me to listen to the Lord and give His Word to someone. I was nervous, but I did it.

Afterward, one of the leaders came up to me and told me that I had done it wrong. I had not used the proper formal language that should accompany a Prophetic message such as, "Thus says the Lord." I was taken aback. That is not how I speak. It took me a long time to get over those words.

God had to show me that He gives me the words, and I am to say what He gives me to say no matter how I feel about it or how I believe others will think about it.

The way to get over this is to know what God thinks of you. When you accept that you are completely loved just the way you are and that He has a unique purpose for your life, it frees you from others' opinions.

Now that does not mean that you cannot accept the positive words spoken over you. The Lord will send His people to encourage you, and you need to receive those words with joy.

Not Being Honest With Ourselves

Some Christians are "insane." Now before you get mad at me, one of the definitions of insanity is doing the same thing repeatedly and expecting a different result. They are unwilling to give up the bad things in their lives, but they expect God to bless them. They refuse to look into the mirror and examine themselves. They are not honest with themselves, with God or with others.

There is work that God expects us to do. He is not a fairy who waves a magic wand and poof; things disappear out of our lives. We are the ones who have to grow in Him through prayer, reading the Word, worship and obedience to what God says.

As you can see, there are many ways that your intimacy with God can be blocked, but I have good news for you! In the next chapter, I will show you a way to blow all those blockages away.

Our mistakes will become a learning process for miracles and our tests becomes testimonies.

- Pastor Zak

Chapter 5: Intimacy & The Baptism Of The Holy Spirit

*But you will receive power when the Holy
Spirit has come upon you; and you shall
be My witnesses both in Jerusalem, and in
all Judea and Samaria, and even to the
remotest part of the earth.*

Acts 1:8

The disciples were not sure what was going to happen. The last two months had been the most incredible time of their life. Jesus had been crucified, buried and raised from the dead. He had appeared to them several times after that and then was taken up into heaven. He left them the instructions to wait in Jerusalem until the Holy Spirit came upon them.

They had joy and anticipation in their hearts but also fear. They were missing their Lord. The Pharisee's (the ruling priests of Israel) had killed Jesus, and now that the news that He was raised from the dead was spreading, they were looking to take out the disciples too.

Peter would have been missing his best friend and the close companionship they had. He had failed Jesus once; he would not do it again. If Jesus told them to wait in Jerusalem, Peter would do it, even if it cost him his life. So, they waited.

When the day of Pentecost came, and the Holy Spirit filled them, they finally understood why Jesus had to go back to heaven. Instead of only a few being able to be close to God, now anyone who received Christ as Saviour could experience His love.

The Holy Spirit's Roles

Even though this chapter is about baptism by the Holy Spirit, there are a few things I want to make clear, as they are areas where new believers get confused. First, it is the Holy Spirit that comes into you at salvation. The Holy Spirit resides in your heart and spirit when you are saved, but that is not the baptism of the Holy Spirit.

Second, only those who are saved can be baptized in the Holy Ghost. This baptism is not for unbelievers. Often, those who are not saved will feel and react to the Holy Spirit's presence as He woos them to come to Jesus, but that is not the same as baptism.

The Holy Spirit has several roles, but two of the most important is to bring you to Jesus. He is the go-between, between you and God. It is Him that you feel when you sense that God is near. The Holy Spirit shows you how to bring glory to God.

His second role is to love you, convict you and teach you as a born-again Christian. The Holy Spirit speaks to your spirit and tells you things and He is the one that you feel when you are about to do something that you know you should not. He also makes the Word of God make sense and opens up your eyes so that you can receive spiritual things.

What Does It Mean To Be Baptized In The Spirit?

God is the God of gifts, and the baptism of the Holy Spirit is a gift He offers freely to all born-again believers. God does not want to just be a part of your life. He wants to overflow in your life. God wants His presence to be so real and to empower you to do things you never thought possible. He wants to use you to make a more significant impact on this world.

But...

God is a gentleman and never forces you to do anything. That is why the Holy Spirit baptism is a gift. You must want and ask for it. You are choosing to allow God to have more control in your life and become a willing vessel in His hands.

Does that mean that if you are not baptized in the Holy Spirit, the Lord cannot use you? Of course not. I know many Godly brothers and sisters in the Lord that He uses without them being filled with the Holy Ghost. God uses whom He chooses, and it is not up to us to decide who is fit or not.

Even Jesus knew that he had to be baptized in the Spirit. God, who came to earth in the form of a man, needed the Spirit's help while in human form.

In Luke 3:21 and 4:1-2 NASB, John writes,

> *Now when all the people were baptized, Jesus was also baptized, and while He was praying, heaven was opened, and the Holy Spirit descended upon Him in bodily form like a dove, and a voice came out of heaven, "You are My beloved Son, in You I am well-pleased.*
>
> *Jesus, full of the Holy Spirit, returned from the Jordan and was led around by the Spirit in the wilderness for forty days, being tempted by the devil.*

So, my question to you is, if Jesus needed the Holy Spirit to empower Him, how much more do we need the Holy Spirit? There has been much false teaching going around saying that the baptism of the Holy Spirit ended with the disciples and that it was only intended for that dispensation. I can tell you with all assurance that the Holy Spirit is still moving in power today!

How Do You Get Baptized In The Holy Spirit?

It is straightforward. It is just like salvation; you ask for it and then believe that you have received it. You can say a simple prayer like this.

Jesus, I thank You for Your love and the wonderful gifts that You give us. I surrender my life to You and ask You to baptize me in the Holy Spirit and fill me to overflowing. I receive it now.

You will see the evidence of it when you start speaking in tongues or other languages.

I have seen many people struggle with the receiving part of the Baptism. They pray, and then nothing seems to happen, and then they get disappointed. There are many reasons for that.

First, some learn that it does not exist anymore, so there is a war between their spirit and mind. Their spirit wants it, but their mind tells them it is not possible. The baptism is something you accept by faith. As soon as you pray it, you are baptized no matter what seems to be going on externally.

Some believers may physically react to the infilling of Holy Spirit, but others do not. Neither one is proof that the Spirit is there. We are all unique individuals and how we respond to God is unique as well. If you fall into this group, take time to study the Word and listen to testimonies of those filled with the Spirit. Build up your faith, and when you are ready, open your mouth, start to speak and believe that God will give you what you need.

Second, God does not possess you, take over your body or force you to do things you do not want to do. He is not going to take over your mouth like a puppet and make you say something. If you desire to speak in tongues, you need to start speaking and trust God to give you the words.

You may hear them in your head, and they may sound silly but speak them out. God is developing a new language in you, and you become more fluent in it the more you practice.

Third, it may not come all at once. My friend Kim only got one word when she first got filled with the Holy Ghost. She was faithful to say that one word over and over, then all of a sudden, it was two words and then before you know it, she was speaking in full sentences.

Fourth, never judge yourself by what others can do or experience. God does not have favourites, and even though it may seem like others are doing mighty things for the Lord, it is the small things that sometimes can make the biggest changes. Do not despise the day of small beginnings. Be faithful where you are at now.

Why Does God Want Us To Speak In Tongues?

In Jude 1:20, Paul writes,

> *But you, beloved, building yourselves up on your most holy faith, praying in the Holy Spirit.*

The first and foremost use of speaking in tongues is to build or edify yourself in the Lord. It is a gift that God uses to help you live a holy life. When you speak in tongues, your spirit is speaking, not your mind, will or emotions. That is essential because many times, our thoughts or feelings get in the way of what God wants. Speaking in tongues allows you to pray God's perfect will in every situation.

It also connects you directly with God to feel His presence. If life is not going the way that you think it should, then you can pray in tongues and allow God to minister to you and fill you with peace and joy. It is a beautiful way to communicate with God because the enemy does not understand it and cannot interfere.

I love speaking in tongues, especially when I do not know what to pray. Romans 8:26 NASB says:

In the same way the Spirit also helps our weakness; for we do not know how to pray as we should, but the Spirit Himself intercedes for us with groaning too deep for words.

God even provides for us when we do not know what to say. What an amazing God!

The second use is to minister to the Body of Christ through the gift of speaking in tongues and prophecy, which we will cover in chapter eight.

One question that I get asked a lot is, do I have to be baptized in the Holy Spirit over and over again, or is it a one-time thing? You only need to be saved once. You do not need to keep asking Jesus to save you. He already did that on the cross. The baptism is different. You can and should be refilled many times.

Think of it this way. We are like buckets with holes in them. The holes can come from sin in our lives and they happen as we give out to others. The Holy Spirit is likened to water, and what happens when you fill a bucket with a hole in it? It keeps coming out, and it continually needs refilling.

God loves it when we come to Him and ask Him to fill us over and over again. His heart desires to be in close union with us.

One other important thing to note: The Holy Spirit is the gateway to God's supernatural gifts. You cannot walk in them without being filled with the Holy Spirit.

I want to encourage you. If you have never been baptized in the Holy Spirit, do not wait any longer. My life changed dramatically when the Spirit filled me, and I have never looked back since. It is one of the most wonderful things you can experience in life.

Wow, we are halfway there. In the rest of the book, we will look at the supernatural in our lives and how God wants to use it to help ourselves and others.

Looking at the mirror does not change us, but looking into God, the mirror of God's word does. Glancing into it won't change us. We have to be intentional and look with purpose.

- Pastor Zak

Chapter 6: Prophecy In A Person's Life

For no prophecy was ever made by an act of human will, but men moved by the Holy Spirit spoke from God.

2 Peter 1:21 NASB

Shirley was tired and worn out. She recently saw several significant changes in her life, including losing her job due to a work shortage. Through it all, she prayed, read the Word of God and continued to worship Jesus and was thankful for all He had done in her life. That had sustained her. On this day, though, the weight seemed more than she could bear.

She let her Bible fall open, and she looked down and saw Isaiah 40: 28-31 NASB

Do you not know? Have you not heard?
The Everlasting God, the Lord, the Creator
of the ends of the earth
Does not become weary or tired.
His understanding is inscrutable.
He gives strength to the weary,
And to him who lacks might He increases
power.
Though youths grow weary and tired,
And vigorous young men stumble badly,
Yet those who wait for the Lord
Will gain new strength;
They will mount up with wings like eagles,
They will run and not get tired,
They will walk and not become weary.

She smiled, whispered a thank you and got ready for church. The burden on her heart had not completely lifted, but hope was starting to grow.

During the worship at church, she started to feel something strange that she could not describe. She knew it was the Lord but was unsure what it meant. When the Pastor began to preach, he read those same verses from Isaiah, and her heart began to leap. She knew that God cared about her and what was going on. Joy began to fill her heart, but anticipation and apprehension were there too.

The Pastor looked right at her as he invited the congregation up to the altar to receive ministry and prayer. Shirley had never gone up for prayer before. At other churches she had attended, the assembly was not allowed to approach the altar. Shirley felt the Lord tell her to go up but was afraid of what might happen. She bowed her head quickly and made it look like she was praying, so no one would ask her if she wanted to go up.

The feeling that she needed to go up kept growing, as did the fear. Then suddenly, she heard the still small voice of the Lord say, "Trust me, Shirley. Take that one small step of faith. I will not let you down." She got up quickly and practically ran to the altar before she could change her mind.

A woman stepped up to her and said, "Shirley, you were reading Isaiah 40 this morning before you came to church, right?" Shirley could not believe it. How could this woman know that? "The Lord told me to tell you that He has seen your faithfulness to Him and is pleased with you. He has a plan in place that will bring you through this time of trial and testing. Tomorrow, He is going to tell you to do something, and you are to do it immediately."

Tears formed in Shirley's eyes, and she thanked the woman for what she had said and returned to her seat.

On Monday, she was driving her car to get groceries, and as she passed a particular store, she felt like she should stop and go in. Remembering what the lady had said to her the day before, she turned into the parking lot, got out and walked in.

She had never been to this store before, but she immediately liked it. It carried fine clothing, jewelry, accessories and some art. Shirley had a degree in fine arts and was well versed in fabrics and what looked good on people. She had dreamed of working in a place like this.

She started walking around and noticed a young woman looking at three different dresses to figure out which one was best. There did not seem to be any employees anywhere, so Shirley sauntered over there and said, "I think the bright purple one would look great with your dark complexion." The young woman thanked her and took it to the dressing room to try it on. She came out smiling, wearing the purple dress, and Shirley nodded at her.

Shirley had not realized that the store owner Patricia had been watching. She came over to Shirley and asked how she could help her, and Shirley replied, "I just came in to look around. You look so sad, what happened?" Tears started to roll down Patricia's face as she said, "A couple of months ago, my best employee and good friend came down sick and within a week was gone, and since then I haven't been able to find anyone that could come close to doing what she did. She was the heart of this store. I saw you helping that young woman. You have a good eye and a kind heart. You don't need a job, do you?"

Now tears started to come down Shirley's face. "Yes, I do." She told Patricia about losing her job and how hard it had been. Patricia looked at her and asked her when she could start, and Shirley answered, "Right now." Patricia smiled and said, "That is great. Let me take care of this customer, and then we can do your paperwork."

Shirley stood there, amazed and thankful for what the Lord had done. (This was another God Moment happening. For sure!) That moment turned into a full-time job that eventually ended up with her owning the store when Patricia retired, and it all began with a word from the Lord.

What Is Prophecy?

Simply, it is a communication from God to man, and it can take several forms. It can be something you read in the Bible that pops into your eyes and comes alive. It may be a Scripture that you have read many times, but all of a sudden, it has a deeper meaning or a direct application to your life at this moment.

It can also be something that God directly speaks to your heart, or it can be something that God speaks to you through another person.

The goal is for you to hear from the Lord to:

- Give you direction
- Convict you when you are doing something wrong
- Protect you from making mistakes
- Show you how to pray for others and give words of wisdom and knowledge to them
- Inspire you

Before Jesus came into my room that first night, I didn't even know that God spoke. To find out that not only does God love me, but He wanted to talk to me was one of the most incredible experiences of my life.

I remember the first time someone gave me a Prophetic word. A gentleman had called me up and told me things about myself that he had no way of knowing. Then he said to me that one day, I would preach around the world and plant churches. I would also prophesy! It inspired me to draw close to God and start moving slowly in that direction. Now that is the life that I live.

God created us to hear His voice. In John 10:2-5 NASB, Jesus says,

> *But he who enters by the door is a shepherd*
> *of the sheep. To him the doorkeeper opens,*
> *and the sheep hear his voice, and he calls his*
> *own sheep by name and leads them out.*
> *When he puts forth all his own, he goes*

ahead of them, and the sheep follow him because they know his voice. A stranger they simply will not follow, but will flee from him, because they do not know the voice of strangers.

In Bible times, shepherds would put their sheep all together in a corral at night for protection, and someone would watch the gate, so no one but the shepherds could get in. In the morning, the shepherds would come and call out to their sheep, and only their sheep would go to them. They knew and only trusted the voice of their master and would not come for another.

Those who know God have learned to hear His voice and follow Him.

People have complicated prophecy so that we are either afraid of it or do not understand its role in our lives. Many churches have made it something that only the 'super-spiritual' can access, which is not the truth. From God's perspective prophecy was designed to encourage and build you up in Him. God wants to be close to you. He wants you to experience His love in many ways. Prophecy is a gift He gives you to allow you to know that He cares and wants the very best for you.

Simple Prophecy And Prophetic Ministry

As Christians, there is much confusion between simple prophecy and the role and office of the prophet. They are very different, and I hope that this section will clear this up.

> *But the one who prophesies speaks to people*
> *for edification, exhortation, and consolation.*

1 Corinthians 14:3 NASB

First, what is a simple prophecy? It is a word of encouragement or comfort that the Lord will give to a Christian to speak to someone else, including the unsaved. It can include details that the Lord may reveal to the person giving the prophecy to prove that it is real. These words are designed to edify, build up the other person or witness to them, and any Christian can give them.

Then there is the role of a Prophet. A Prophet has grown in the Lord and has proven their trustworthiness, and God equips them to give deeper level prophecies, especially in the church. These words can be directional and also corrective. They do not tear someone down but bring them to repentance and healing.

These words are called a Word of Prophecy and can be given during a service or ministry time. People who provide these words function in the Spiritual Gifts. They are a vital part of the church as they have become skilled in hearing from the Lord, but they still do not walk in the office of a prophet.

Someone who walks in the office of a prophet does so as their primary ministry. In Ephesians 4:11 NASB, it says,

*And He gave some as apostles, and
some as prophets, and some as evangelists,
and some as Pastors and teachers.*

The office of a Prophet is a calling that God has placed on someone's life. This person hears very direct words for leaders of churches, ministries, nations and countries, and is considered to be the mouthpiece of God, in a sense. They walk closely and humbly before God.

A Warning

You must consider any Prophetic word carefully, especially if you are new to receiving them. Any directional words such as, "Marry this person, move to a certain place, take a certain job," must be taken to the Lord and have it confirmed before acting upon it.

First of all, we are human, and we make mistakes and can say the wrong thing. Secondly, not all Prophetic words ARE FOR NOW! Some are to plant a seed for the future and for you to pray, trust and bring into existence.

I have known people who heard that they were to be a missionary and sold everything and moved to a new country without seeking confirmation first. Prophetic words should confirm what the Lord has already told you. If it does not, you need to take it to the Lord in prayer and seek counsel from your Pastor or another mature Christian.

Many Ways To Hear From God

I love how creative God is and the many ways that He can communicate with us. The first and foremost is through the Bible, but it is not the only way. God can speak to your heart and mind, or you can hear His audible voice. He can speak to you through a dream, a friend, or even a stranger who may come up to you and say something. They may not even know that they are prophesying to you. Sometimes, it can be nature.

The heavens are telling of the glory of God; and their expanse is declaring the work of His hands.

Psalm 19:1

I have even had God speak to me through a billboard once. There is one essential component. You need to spend time listening to God. That is the only way to hear His voice. Your relationship with Him needs to take priority in your life. You will hear me say that many times in this book. I cannot stress it enough. There is no magical formula to hearing from God. You must spend the time with Him and attune your spirit to hear His voice only and no other, and prophecy is one of the main ways that God speaks to you.

In the next chapter, we will focus on how to minister to others in the Prophetic. God wants to speak to you every day, but some of the words He gives you will be for others, and you need to know how to walk in that.

Nothing can stop you when God is on your side. You will be unstoppable. Get ready for a season of personal Revival.

- Pastor Zak

Chapter 7: Ministering To Others In The Prophetic

Anything you do in this life that is lined up
with God's will is never about you. Take
courage and trust in Him.

Pastor Zak

As we begin this chapter, I want to share a testimony from Pastor Jerry Steingard.

In August of 2013, Zak called me on the telephone to give me a word he believed the Lord had given him for me:

"Jubilee Christian Fellowship (which is our church family that we were attending at the time, in Stratford, Ontario), would be asking me to Pastor the church again. And WHEN (not if) they did, I should not automatically reply by saying 'no,' but pray about it and if I said 'yes,' there would be much healing and blessing for everyone."

My immediate response to Zak was one of skepticism, "Zak, you have given me many significant and encouraging words from the Lord over the years, but this time you are definitely off. There is no way the church is going to ask me to be their Pastor (again)!"

Zak again conveyed to me that "when" they asked me, I should not give a flat 'no' response.

At that time, my wife and I had zero interest in Pastoring a congregational church again. For the previous ten years, we had given our time and attention to Pastoring a network of house churches, and Zak was aware of that fact. Despite this being the case in the natural, Zak was confident that this was the Lord speaking through him.

A month later, Zak phoned me up again and asked, "Has the church asked you yet?"

And I responded with, "Of course not Zak. There's no way they are going to ask me to Pastor them again. You have missed it on this one, Zak!"

Another month passed, and Zak called me for a third time with the same question, and I gave the same answer.

But two weeks later, the elder/board of Jubilee called me up and asked for me to come to their elders' meeting later that week. At that meeting, they asked me if my wife, Pam, and I would pray about becoming Jubilee's interim Pastor. I immediately replied that I would be willing to do so. They were quite shocked at my answer and said, "Shouldn't you and your wife pray about it first?"

I said, "Actually, we have been praying for the last three months now, and we feel the Lord has done a work in our hearts so that we are willing to say 'yes,' if asked to do so."

The next day, a Sunday, the eldership announced that I would be their interim Pastor, effective immediately. And it turned out exactly as the Lord had promised, a real blessing and healing for everyone concerned over the next three years! After passing the baton over to my younger assistant Pastor three years later, I continue to be part of the Pastoral team and see the Lord do amazing things in and through this growing and thriving apostolic church (founded by John and Carol Arnott)!

I highly value the Prophetic gift in my life, and I am so thankful to Zak, not only for his friendship over the years but for his bold and persistent Prophetic encouragement to my family and me! Praise God that He still speaks to His sheep in our day, whether it be directly to us or through one of His servants, the prophets!

One of the main reasons why the Church is ineffective today in reaching a lost world is they try to do it in their strength or do not do it because they are afraid.

It makes me sad and frustrated at the same time because God not only wants us to reach out but equips us to do so.

The Other Role Of Prophecy

The gift of prophecy has different levels. In the last chapter, we looked at how a person can use prophecy in their own lives. This chapter will focus on how God uses prophecy in the Church and to a lost world.

First of all, Jesus is the head of the Body of Christ,

> *And He put all things in subjection under His feet, and gave Him as head over all things to the church, which is His body, the fullness of Him who fills all in all.*
>
> *Ephesians 1:22-23 NASB*

Besides the Word of God, prophecy, and some of the other spiritual gifts is the way that Jesus communicates and leads His church. Not every situation we run into in life has specific directions in the Bible. That is why Pastors and Church leadership must hear directly from the Holy Spirit for guidance.

Does that mean that those who are not in leadership do not need to hear for themselves? No, there are many people out there who need to hear from God that your Pastor will never reach, but you will.

Second, God wants you to not only hear for yourself but others as well. There is a progression to this. You must first learn to hear for yourself and be obedient to what you are told before God will trust you to speak to others. It all comes down to how intimate you are with Jesus.

As your relationship grows, the Lord will ask you to do something or share something with another person. It may come as an idea while you are reading God's word or praying. It can also come as an impression in your heart, a feeling that you should do something, or you may hear the voice of the Lord audibly. However, God speaks to you, it is essential to obey, even if it may seem foolish or weird.

Not too long ago, while I was leading a church service, I felt impressed to say a specific word. I was not sure why I needed to say it, but I did. It turned out that there was a visitor in the church, and that was her last name. She was amazed God had mentioned her in the church; my wife Karen-Marie led her to the Lord afterwards.

Prophecy is an effective witnessing tool to let people know that God is with them.

Third, God wants to encourage, instruct, correct and equip His saints, and He does that through prophecy and the gifts of the Holy Spirit, which we will cover in the next chapter.

Many times, over the years, I have either given a prophecy in church or heard a word in the church that has changed lives. When God speaks to the heart in this way, it is powerful. Sometimes we feel weak, and we do not want to tell others, yet the Lord loves us and wants to show it by giving someone a word for the church and knowing that it is for them.

Chapter 8: The Gifts of The Holy Spirit In Action

Now concerning spiritual gifts, brethren, I do not want you to be unaware. Now there are varieties of gifts, but the same Spirit. And there are varieties of ministries, and the same Lord. There are varieties of effects, but the same God who works all things in all persons.

1 Corinthians 12:1, 4-6 NASB

Daniel's heart was heavy and broken as he sat in church with his wife. That week they had miscarried their second baby. He thought that losing the first baby was hard but now a second one?

He kept wondering what he had done wrong; did he somehow cause this? Did he sin, and now the baby was dead. As he looked over at his wife, tears started to form, making him feel even worse. He was supposed to be his family's spiritual head, and he could not even comfort his wife.

What made matters worse is that they had both agreed that they would not tell anyone. They were ashamed and did not want to answer questions about why it happened, nor did they want everyone offering condolences.

As worship was ending, one of the elders stood up and said, "The Lord has laid on my heart today that there is a couple here who has just experienced a miscarriage. Your hearts are broken, and you are feeling too ashamed to tell anyone. The Lord wants you to know you have nothing to be ashamed of, and He is holding your child in His hands right now. If you continue to turn to Him, He will come in and heal your heart and give you peace."

Daniel and his wife looked at each other. How could he have known? The only people they had told were their unsaved parents who lived hours away. They felt the presence of God and a holy warmth came over their bodies. At the altar call, they both went up and told the Pastor what had happened. He prayed with them, and they left with a peace in their hearts that helped carry them through this season.

Are The Gifts Real?

Yes, they are. There is much erroneous teaching out there that says that the gifts ended with the Apostles and that this current move of the Spirit is fake, but it is not.

Throughout history, you can find the gifts in use. There are times when the usage of the gift has been small, but they were still there. I believe that this current move of the Holy Spirit is what is prophesied in Joel 2: 28-29 NASB:

> *"It will come about after this*
> *That I will pour out My Spirit on all*
> *mankind; and your sons and daughters will*
> *prophesy,*
> *Your old men will dream dreams,*
> *Your young men will see visions.*
> *Even on the male and female servants*
> *I will pour out My Spirit in those days."*

In God's Word, He says He never changes, so if the first century Christians needed the Holy Spirit to live successfully, how much more do we need Him in these end times?

If the gifts were only for the first generation of Christians, then why does Paul write chapters about using the gifts in the Book of Corinthians if they were going to pass away soon? Our God is a good Father who knows what we need, and those gifts are vital today.

There are three main reasons why God gave the gifts. The first is to encourage His body, the Church.

But God has so composed the body, giving more abundant honor to that member which lacked, so that there may be no division in the body, but that the members may have the same care for one another. And if one member suffers, all the members suffer with it; if one member is honored, all the members rejoice with it.

1 Corinthians 12:24-26 NASB

The gifts allow us to care for one another and build each other up. The second is for the Church to run effectively. We need God's direction and wisdom to guide the Church as a whole, and our lives personally. The Bible uses two words for the Word; Logos and Rhema. Logos is the written Word of God, the Bible. It mirrors what our lives should look like; it is God's love letter to us. Rhema is God's word for right now, and it can be different for each person.

For example: let's say God told your whole Church to go three hours away to another city. How would each member get there? There are hundreds of ways. That is where Rhema comes in. God may tell one person to walk to the car rental place and rent a car because the person behind the counter needs to hear about Jesus. God may tell one person to stop at a particular fast-food place because an accident would have happened if they stayed on the road. Another person may be told to wait two more days before leaving because God wants them to do things before, they go. They all end up doing what God said, but how they did it was different.

Third, it is a tool to witness to the unsaved. The unsaved will be drawn to God when they see the supernatural. When Jesus told the woman at the well about her life, she knew He was God, so she ran back to her town and told others.

How Can You Walk In The Gifts?

There is one prerequisite to using the gifts – you must be saved and sanctified by the blood of Jesus. You must have asked Him to come into your heart and forgive you for all your sins and have accepted His forgiveness. Once that happens, the Holy Spirit comes in, and He activates the gifts in your life as He chooses (and the first one is usually faith, which we will talk about later in the chapter.)

Now there are varieties of gifts, but the same Spirit. And there are varieties of ministries, and the same Lord. There are varieties of effects, but the same God who works all things in all persons. But to each one is given the manifestation of the Spirit for the common good. For to one is given the word of wisdom through the Spirit, and to another the word of knowledge according to the same Spirit; to another faith by the same Spirit,

*and to another gifts of healing by the one
Spirit, and to another the effecting
of miracles, and to another prophecy, and to
another the distinguishing of spirits, to
another various kinds of tongues, and to
another the interpretation of tongues. But
one and the same Spirit works all these
things, distributing to each one individually
just as He wills.*

1 Corinthians 12:4-11 NASB

What about the baptism of the Holy Spirit?
Where does that fit? Some believe you need to be
baptized in the Holy Ghost to walk in the gifts. I do
not believe that is true. When you are saved, you
receive the Holy Spirit. For me, it comes down to
your ability to use the gifts.

When you are baptized in the Holy Spirit, you
yield yourself to God and allow Him to use you as
He sees fits. You become a willing tool in the hands
of the Master, and that is why you see the gifts
manifested more in those baptized in the Holy
Spirit.

The Gifts Of The Holy Spirit

The Scripture above lists nine gifts, and we will
cover eight of them here as we have already covered
the role of prophecy. These are not the only gifts. As
you read through the New Testament, you will see
many others, including ministering gifts such as

mercy, administration and hospitality, but this chapter will focus on the supernatural gifts.

The Word Of Knowledge

The word of knowledge is the ability to know a fact about a situation or a person that could not have been known by natural means, only divine ones.

This gift allows a person to see what God sees about another person. There was one time I felt the Lord tell me to say the word, "Washroom." I did not know why I was to say it, but it turned out that a woman in the service had been praying to God to confirm her healing and asked Him to have someone say the word "Washroom" to her.

In the Bible, Jesus used this gift many times, including John 1:48 NASB with Nathaniel.

> *Nathanael said to Him, "How do You know me?" Jesus answered and said to him, "Before Philip called you, when you were under the fig tree, I saw you."*

The Word of Wisdom

It is a word that God gives you to solve problems divinely. For example, when Solomon ruled as king, two women came before him:

> *The one woman said, "Oh, my Lord, this woman and I live in the same house; and I gave birth to a child while she was in the house. It happened on the third day after I*

93

gave birth, that this woman also gave birth to a child, and we were together. There was no stranger with us in the house, only the two of us in the house. This woman's son died in the night, because she lay on it. So, she arose in the middle of the night and took my son from beside me while your maidservant slept, and laid him in her bosom, and laid her dead son in my bosom. When I rose in the morning to nurse my son, behold, he was dead; but when I looked at him carefully in the morning, behold, he was not my son, whom I had borne." Then the other woman said, "No! For the living one is my son, and the dead one is your son." But the first woman said, "No! For the dead one is your son, and the living one is my son." Thus, they spoke before the king.

Then the king said, "The one says, 'This is my son who is living, and your son is the dead one'; and the other says, 'No! For your son is the dead one, and my son is the living one.' The king said, "Get me a sword." So, they brought a sword before the king. The king said, "Divide the living child in two, and give half to the one and half to the other." Then the woman whose child was the living one spoke to the king, for she was deeply stirred over her son and said, "Oh, my lord, give her the living child, and by no means kill him." But the other said, "He shall be neither mine nor yours; divide him!" Then the king said, "Give the first woman the living child, and by no means kill him. She is his mother." When all Israel heard of the judgment which the king

*had handed down, they feared the king,
for they saw that the wisdom of God was in
him to administer justice.*

1 Kings 3: 17-28 NASB

There was no way for Solomon to know who the baby belonged to, but God gave him the wisdom to figure it out.

The Gift Of Faith

Everyone who is saved has a measure of faith. The Bible makes it clear that:

*For by grace you have
been saved through faith; and that not of
yourselves, it is the gift of God.*

Ephesians 2:8 NASB

As your relationship with the Lord grows, so does your faith so that you can believe God for bigger and bigger things. Many times, these things are impossible without the direct intervention of God.

I have known many people who have believed God for big things in their life, including spouses, children, homes, dream jobs, travel and ministry, and many other things that have come to pass.

The gift of faith requires time. Not everything that you believe God for happens immediately.

The Gift Of Healing

It is a supernatural enhancement given to believers through the Holy Spirit to minister various physical healing and restoration to others. The Holy Spirit will lead you to who to pray for and when. It is directed and guided by God.

There was one time I was with a gentleman who was experiencing severe hearing loss. I felt the Holy Ghost tell me to lay hands on the man and command him to be healed. When I did, he was able to hear again.

The gift of healing is also a great witnessing tool as those around the person who got healed see God's power.

The Working Of Miracles

This gift is humanly impossible but divinely simple. Where the gift of faith can take time, the working of miracles is immediate. It is the ability to do something beyond the normal scope of human ability. A great example of a miracle was Jesus' first miracle when He turned the water into wine.

The Gift Of Discerning Of Spirits

Discerning can describe the process of determining God's desire in a situation or a person's life or identifying the true nature of a thing, whether it is from God, people or the devil.

For example, there have been times that I have looked at a person and was able to determine that they were under the influence of an evil spirit. Once that demon was released from the person, they could accept what God wanted to give them.

The Gift Of Tongues

There are two types of tongues, the one we use personally in prayer or praise to God and then the gift of tongues, which is a Prophetic message given in an earthly or heavenly language inspired by the Holy Spirit for the church.

You see, this happens most often during a church service, and it needs to be interpreted so that the congregation can benefit from it.

Occasionally God has used it as a witnessing tool. When someone in the congregation does not speak the same language as the main one spoken or speaks in more than one language, God may give a message in another earthly language that only that person or a small group of people understand in order to tell them something. Many times, these people are unsaved and get saved by it.

The Gift Of Interpreting Tongues

This gift is tied to the last one and is used as a supernatural sign to both believers and non-believers alike. When a message is given in tongues, someone needs to interpret it for the Body of Christ to be edified. It can be the same person who gave the message or someone else.

How They Are To Be Seen

Here is one of the key points about the gifts. They are not proof of spiritual maturity, and you should not see believers who use gifts as more important because God chooses to use them. We are all the same in Christ, sinners saved by grace. No one is more special or more loved than any other.

If someone makes you feel inferior because they can do something in the Lord that you cannot, forgive them and pray for them that God will remove that spirit of pride from them.

We are all called to walk humbly before God, recognizing that anything good inside of us comes from Him, and it is not of ourselves. It is not something to be boastful about but humbled and thankful that the Lord loves us.

Also, not all gifts demonstrate to the world the power of God but are vital to the body like hospitality, mercy, teaching, evangelism and administration gifts. All these gifts are needed for the church to function well.

For even as the body is one and yet has many members, and all the members of the body, though they are many, are one body, so also is Christ.

*For by one Spirit we were all baptized into
one body, whether Jews or Greeks, whether
slaves or free, and we were all made to drink
of one Spirit.*

*For the body is not one member, but many.
If the foot says, "Because I am not a hand, I
am not a part of the body," it is not for this
reason any the less a part of the body. And if
the ear says, "Because I am not an eye, I am
not a part of the body," it is not for this
reason any the less a part of the body. If the
whole body were an eye, where would the
hearing be? If the whole were hearing,
where would the sense of smell be? But now
God has placed the members, each one of
them, in the body, just as He desired. If they
were all one member, where would the body
be? But now there are many members, but
one body.*

*And the eye cannot say to the hand, "I have
no need of you"; or again the head to the
feet, "I have no need of you." On the
contrary, it is much truer that the members
of the body which seem to be weaker are
necessary; and those members of the body
which we deem less honorable, on these we
bestow more abundant honor, and our less
presentable members become much more
presentable, whereas our more presentable
members have no need of it. But God
has so composed the body, giving more
abundant honor to that member which
lacked, so that there may be no division in*

the body, but that the members may have the same care for one another.

And if one member suffers, all the members suffer with it; if one member is honored, all the members rejoice with it. Now you are Christ's body, and individually members of it.

1 Corinthians 12:12-27

God makes it very clear in His word that all members of the Body of Christ are to be treated with honour and respect.

In the next chapter, we will focus on how the prophetic gift and the other gifts should be used in the church.

Chapter 9: The Rules To The Prophetic

What is the outcome then, brethren? When you assemble, each one has a psalm, has a teaching, has a revelation, has a tongue, has an interpretation. Let all things be done for edification. If anyone speaks in a tongue, it should be by two or at the most three, and each in turn, and one must interpret; but if there is no interpreter, he must keep silent in the church; and let him speak to himself and to God. Let two or three prophets speak, and let the others pass judgment. But if a revelation is made to another who is seated, the first one must keep silent. For you can all prophesy one by one, so that all may learn and all may be exhorted; and the spirits of prophets are

subject to prophets; for God is not a
God of confusion but of peace, as in all the
churches of the saints.

1 Corinthians 14:26-33

I have learned as a Pastor that when it comes to the prophetic gift of God, there is much confusion on the usage of it. I have seen both extremes where people will not use it because they are afraid of it, to the point that they abuse it and do not follow the rules. I hope that this chapter brings clarity and allows you to walk in all the gifts properly.

The prophetic is something that you grow in. You start out like a baby, learning how to walk. You need a seasoned person in the prophetic helping you, encouraging you and training you. It was the same when you became a born-again Christian. You did not know all the ins and outs of this new life.

It is a learning process, like a little kid learning how to ride a bicycle; sometimes you fall, sometimes you get up, sometimes you hurt yourself. The key is walking with somebody else who can guide you, help direct you, give you some guidance, and navigate you.

One of the best ways to start is by watching. Go to a church where the prophetic is operating and learn. The most significant part of the prophetic is your relationship with God. You must always stay humble before Him. Walking in the prophetic is not a spiritual badge that makes you more special, more loved or better than anyone else. Just remember that God used a donkey to prophesy. Stay in God's Word, pray continually, confess your sins to the Lord and when required to others. Remember that you are only the tool of the Lord, and He is the One that gets all the glory.

If you feel like God has given you a word for someone, here is the way to go about it. The first step is to go to a trusted prophetic person or Pastor and talk to them about it. If they feel that the word is from God, then go to the person. Tell them that you are learning to walk in the prophetic, and you think that you might have a word for them. Ask them if they are okay with you giving the word to them. If they say, "Yes," give it to them and if they say, "No," then respect them and let it go.

Never go and prophesy over somebody without asking their permission first. Even those who have been doing this for years and years and years, are still growing and learning. It is always a learning process.

The same principles apply when you feel like you have a word for a church. If you are new at giving a prophetic Word, write it out and give it to the Pastor to check over first. However, if you can go to the Pastor and tell him/her what you want to say, then the Pastor can decide whether or not you should give the word to the church.

There will be times when that word is burning in you, and you feel like you must blurt it out. Don't. Always get permission first. Understand that we are human, and we make mistakes. No word from the Lord spoken through a human is 100% correct. There is always a bit of us in there that can get it wrong.

Now, you may be thinking, "But the Spirit is so strong on me, my body is reacting, and I have to say it." Remember what it says in 1 Corinthians 14:32-33 NASB

And the spirits of prophets are subject to prophets; for God is not a God of confusion but of peace, as in all the churches of the saints.

You can control yourself.

Jennifer told me about one of the first times she wanted to prophesy in her church. The Spirit was upon her powerfully, and she had something she wanted to say. She was not sure if it was correct, so she went up to the Pastor's wife and told her, and it was a good thing she did. The first part was right, but Jennifer had added an interpretation based on her own hurts and pains that was not part of what God had given her to say. Jennifer gave the first part and it ministered to someone powerfully. She learned a valuable lesson that day and that is to be careful to only give what God is saying and not add your own thoughts to it.

Rules To The Prophetic

There three goals of prophecy, exhortation, edification and comfort. If the word you get does not fit in one of those three categories, it is best for a novice not to express it. The Prophetic in the church, is for building up, not tearing down. Yes, there can be an element of correction in the prophetic, but that is up to the Lord to bring conviction on someone, not the novice.

Sometimes correction needs to come but should only be done by someone who walks in the office of the prophet and has proven themselves faithful in it. If you are beginning in the prophetic, and feel a strong word of correction, it is either coming from yourself or from the enemy.

Here are some general rules to help you. It is simple: no babies, no dates, no mate, no directional words, and no direct mandates from God. No dates mean that you do not prophesy over people that this person will marry that person, that woman will marry that guy. No babies mean you are not going to prophesy that someone is going to have children.

We cannot say that is the Lord because we could get it wrong and have disastrous effects in a person's life including turning away from God. There may come a time when you have grown in the prophetic that you are ready for those types of words, but not in the beginning.

Here is another thing about the prophetic. Not everything you receive is to be said. Many times, God gives me something so that I can pray for them. When you get a word, ask God what you should do with it. If you do not get an answer, then pray until you do. Not everything with God is right now. Many times, you wait.

The rules are there for a reason. The prophetic, when misused can hurt people and churches. That is why Paul writes several chapters in 1 Corinthians on how the church's prophetic gift functions. God is a God of order, not chaos. The Corinthian church was out of control. Everyone was trying to talk over everyone else, it was like a group of kids who all want their parent's attention all at the same time. Remember, love should always be at the core of what we do.

The Tests Of God

If you want to walk in the gifts of God, you will be tested on it. When you are in school and want to go to the next grade, you have to pass tests. When you are in the Prophetic and want the deeper things, there are tests too. These tests help you grow into a person that can be trusted by the Lord with bigger things.

We will cover several tests but let us focus on the two biggest ones first: submission and obedience. They are the biggest because they deal with two areas that we, as humans, struggle with the most; pride and fear.

The submission test works against our pride and our need to be validated and approved of. It comes down to three areas: what do you do when someone authority above you says, "No, you cannot give that word," or the person you want to give it to refuses you, or someone else gives the word that you were going to give.

What do you do when those things happen? How do you deal with it? You recognize that your only responsibility is to offer to give the message or share your gift. If someone says no, you have done what you need to do, and the responsibility is now on them.

Sometimes God has someone say no to you as a test. Are you going to submit, or are you going to rebel, against the authority in place? You cannot take offence when the person above you does not let you give the word. Those above you know more than you do, and there may be a reason why now is not time to give it out.

When someone else gives the word that you had or reads the word that you submitted, without giving credit to you, what do you do? The point is to have the word go out, and all the credit and glory need to go to God, not you, so it does not matter who gives it.

If you find that your feelings are getting hurt, then that is an area that God needs to come in and heal. You should never give a word to get the glory; if that is your purpose, then you fail the test. Your self-worth is based on what God says about you, not what people say about you.

Tests help mature you in the Holy Spirit and grow you into a person that the Lord can trust with more responsibility. It is not always easy, especially when you feel that others (who you know do not deserve it), get attention and you do not.

Your motive should always be to have the Lord's will done. As you give up your will, you will learn that what He has given you is enough, even if you do not get any recognition for it.

There was a time that the Lord gave me a word for a particular church. I gave the word to the Pastor of that church and he said I could not give the word publicly. But he went ahead anyway and gave the word to the church that the Lord had told me to speak to the church.

I was not angry, I submitted it to him, and he determined whether it should be said or not. It was not my word to begin with, it was Gods. If the other Pastor did something wrong, then that is between him and God. My responsibility was done.

The obedience test; will you do what the Lord is asking you to do, no matter how uncomfortable it will make you? I remember one time I did not have much money. The Lord told me to give my last $100 because the church was contributing money for somebody to buy a house. I struggled with that. Maybe that day I would not have enough food to eat, but that day, because I was obedient and did it, when I went home, in my Bible, there was another $100.

I do not know how it got there, but I know that when I went to church that that day, there was no money in my Bible. Another example for the obedience test is when the Lord asks you to do something that is not in your realm of things that you normally do. If you are obedient to do it, God will always honor his Word because the Bible says obedience is better than sacrifice.

What are some of the other tests you may face? The faith test, the character test and the Scripture test. The faith test is believing that when you did what God has asked you to do, it will work out even when there is no sign of it. The character test is how you react when people do not receive your word well. The Scripture test is ensuring that you quote and give Scripture correctly without offering a commentary on it.

A Few Last Things

You will make mistakes as you grow in walking in the prophetic. Just because you make one mistake does not mean that you should stop. Ask God and the person you gave it to, to forgive you. Put yourself in mentorship under someone who is mature in it. Spend more time in the Word, and prayer, especially tongues.

The prophetic has made a big difference in my life, and I am so thankful for the gifts that God gives. In the last chapter, we will tie everything together, and I will give you some action steps to continue your journey forward.

Chapter 10 – It's Time To Act

*Not that I have already obtained it or have
already become perfect, but I press on so
that I may lay hold of that for which also
I was laid hold of by Christ Jesus. Brethren,
I do not regard myself as having laid hold
of it yet; but one thing I do: forgetting
what lies behind and reaching forward to
what lies ahead, I press on toward the goal
for the prize of the upward call of God
in Christ Jesus.*

Philippians 3:12-14

W hat a journey of love this has been as I
have wanted to write this book for a
long time. I waited on the Lord to see
it come to pass, and now here you are reading the
last chapter. To God, be all the glory!!!

My life has been one adventure after another in the Lord. After I was saved, I had the opportunity to go to Bible School, where I met Karen-Marie, my wife, partner in the ministry, best friend and one that I love with all my heart. She is a blessing in every way in my life, and I am so thankful for her. We also have a wonderful son that I am so proud of. They are gifts from the Lord that fill my life with joy.

The Lord has fulfilled His Prophetic word over me. I have travelled the world preaching the gospel, starting churches and teaching people how to walk in the Holy Spirit. I also Pastor four churches here in my local area.

Like you, I have had good times where my praises rise to the Lord. I had hard times when God wiped away my tears, and I have waited in faith to see His promises come to pass in my life. Throughout it all, I have learned one thing, if I keep my eyes focused on Him, He brings good out of every situation.

And we know that God causes all things to work together for good to those who love God, to those who are called according to His purpose. For those whom He foreknew, He also predestined to become conformed to the image of His Son, so that He would be the firstborn among

many brethren; and these whom
He predestined, He also called; and these
whom He called, He also justified; and these
whom He justified, He also glorified.

Romans 8:28-30, NASB

In this chapter, I want to do two things, share some testimonies of God's supernatural power and give you an action plan to move deeper into the things of God.

Denise Ritchie From Glasgow Scotland

Andrew and I were married in March 1993. We had discussed and agreed that we wanted to have children before we were even engaged, but we were content to enjoy life as a couple for the first four years or so of our marriage.

We then decided it would be a good time to start a family, and we tried to conceive. When a year or so had passed without any success, we attended the doctor, and after a series of tests, they confirmed that we would not conceive naturally. This came as a shock.

As Christians, we believed in a miracle-working God who loves us and wants the best for us, but the 'reality' we were facing seemed overwhelming. As we absorbed our situation, we discussed our options for assisted conception with our consultant. We decided to try an in-vitro fertilization technique as our desire to have a child of our own was strong.

However, as the preparations and consultations progressed, we had a number of questions, some of which had answers that made us uncomfortable. We both firmly believe that God alone should decide when human life begins and ends. We felt that this was not as clear cut with in-vitro fertilization, and we decided that we would opt-out. This was a very difficult and painful decision as this would be giving up on our only chance of conceiving, or so we thought.

Soon after, we decided that we would like to pursue having a family by adoption, recognizing the value of providing a loving home for children who needed it, and acknowledging our desire to parent children whether they were biologically ours or not. We started the assessment to become adoptive parents. This culminated in our approval as adoptive parents two years later, in October 2002, and the wait for children to be placed with us began. However, the adoption was not to be.

Meanwhile, in the summer of 2001, we had met Pastor Zak Gariba, who spent a week staying in our home while he was ministering in Scotland, speaking at home groups and also at Glasgow Elim Pentecostal Church.

While staying with us, Zak shared a prophecy with us in the presence of my sister and brother-in-law that he believed God would give us a child of our own. I will be honest in saying that I did not entirely own this prophecy as I wanted to protect my heart from further pain and disappointment. I suppose I stored it in my heart and waited to see what would happen.

Around two months later, we received a confirmation of this prophecy from another visitor who stayed in our home. Again, I stored it in my heart and waited to see what would happen.

Zak visited us again in November 2002 with his then girlfriend, Karen-Marie. I cannot recall whether he reiterated the prophecy at that time; however, unknown to us I was already pregnant with our daughter, Charis Hope. I only realized this when I looked back at the dates in writing this story. I also realized that Zak's first visit is recorded in our visitor's book as two years to the day before Charis was due to be born.

The name 'Charis' means gift, and we could not have found a more appropriate name. We subsequently went on to have two more daughters truly by the grace of God: Lois Grace and Abigail Peace. I should point out that in previous years I had been walking closely with God; at the time of the prophecies from Zak, I was disobedient to Him in some areas of my life. These three girls are a gift that proves that His promises are true and faithful even when we are not.

Pastor Zak's Side Of The Story

When I came to visit in July 2001, the Lord gave me a word that they would get pregnant; I knew they would, and as I was leaving for the airport, that is when I gave *them the word. As I was about to pray, the Lord told me not to pray for her, because it was him that was the issue. The doctors had tested her but not him. As I prayed for them, I knew it was done.*

When I returned to Scotland from Canada to visit again in November 2002 to have my first date with Karen-Marie, who is now my wife, I stayed with them again, and I stated the prophesy again.

In February 2003, she sent me this email

"This is the email you have been waiting for. I am pregnant."

Eva Hsieh From Taiwan

My husband and I have been married for three years, and we have always wanted to have a baby. We had tried for more than two years, and still nothing. I thought to myself that if we couldn't conceive a baby by the end of 2019, then maybe it was a sign that God wants us to live a life without a child. When Pastor Zak came to Taiwan, it was during my second trial of IVF treatment; I was hopeful and worried. At that time, Pastor Zak prophesied over me that, "It is done in the name of Jesus. When we went back to the hospital to get the results eight days after the convention, Hallelujah I was pregnant!

During my seventh month of pregnancy, the doctor found out that my baby was smaller than she should be. At that time Pastor Zak came to Taiwan again, and he

116

prophesied that "The baby will not be too little and will be healthy. When my baby was born, she was twenty-three percent heavier than expected and very healthy. It was a miracle for us. Praise God.

Testimony Three: Pastor Zak

One day I was cutting my grass when my lawnmower broke. I was not too excited about that, but I decided to buy a new one, since that was old, and I heard the Lord said to me, "No," so I said, "Why?" He told me to wait, so I decided to take it for repair. When I got there, the repairman said it would take a long time (2 months) for it to be done.

My grass was growing taller, I went back to the Lord, and He said, "Wait, I have you covered," so I asked, "What does that mean?" He said the same thing again, so I waited.

In the meantime, my grass was growing taller and taller, my neighbours kept looking at me, and one of them asked if he could lend me a lawnmower, the Lord said, "No." I felt frustrated but kept my cool.

I attended a great conference, and it kept me away during the day from seeing my neighbours. On Saturday evening, as I was praying, the Lord said to me, "I told you to wait; I got it covered." I knew that He meant my Lawn Mower.

During the Sunday Morning service, I took the offering, and I said to the people to have faith and give by faith. *After prayers, I went to sit down, and less than two minutes later, Jon, who is my sound man, came to me and asked if I had ordered a lawnmower. I said, "No," he said that someone is here to deliver a lawnmower. They delivered the lawnmower and left. I asked who had done it; he said he did not ask the person's name, and they were gone.*

I went to look at the lawnmower, it was Lawn Boy, and it was a lime green colour, which is my favourite colour. I knew that it was a gift from the Lord because I never told anyone about my broken lawnmower, and besides that, no one knew that I was at church that morning.

I was astonished about what the Lord could do. Thank you, Jesus.

Your Action Plan

Successfully moving in God's supernatural things is not only based on gifting alone but also having a deep relationship with Him. There have been many Pastors, Evangelists, Prophets and Apostles who have fallen because they got so focused on the gifts of God and how great it made them look that they stopped looking at the One who gave it to them, and as a result, they fell.

Pride kills God in your life.

*Pride goes before destruction, And a haughty
spirit before stumbling.*

Proverbs 16:18

You should never think that anything good in
your life came from you. It came from God's mercy,
grace and love. Not because you deserved it,
because you did not. Jesus died cruelly on the cross,
so that you can have abundant life. Never forget the
price that was paid for you, and walk humbly before
the Lord.

Also, anything you accomplish in God, you did
not do alone. Your family in Christ was praying for
you. Jesus never wanted us to be lone sheep, He
created us to be in community and under authority.
No one person has all the pieces of the puzzle or all
of the gifts (both supernatural and natural). That is
why He puts you into a family of believers for you
to be a part of. You grow and learn from them, and
they grow and learn from you, and together, you
accomplish God's will for your geographic region
and the world.

*So then you are no longer strangers and
aliens, but you are fellow citizens with the
saints, and are of God's household, having
been built on the foundation of the Apostles
and Prophets, Christ Jesus Himself being
the cornerstone, in whom the whole building,*

*being fitted together, is growing into a
holy temple in the Lord, in whom you also
are being built together into a dwelling of
God in the Spirit.*

Ephesians 2: 19-22 NASB

You will have battles in this life that you cannot
fight alone. You will need the prayers of the saints
and the constant presence of the Lord to overcome
the wiles of the enemy. When you walk alone, you
become an easy target for the enemy to take you out
or deceive you. I have seen so many who started out
strong in the Lord but then figured they did not
need others, and now they feel they do not even
need the Lord, nor do they serve Him!

*Be of sober spirit, be on the alert. Your
adversary, the devil, prowls around like a
roaring lion, seeking someone to devour.*

1 Peter 5:8 NASB

When a lion hunts, he does not go for the sheep
in the middle of the group, guarded by the others.
He goes for the sick, the weak and those who stray
too far away from the flock. They are easy pickings.
If you want to stay strong in the Lord, find a good
body of believers to be a part of and be faithful to.
Find a church to belong to that is faithful and
believes the Word of God.

You must also be content where you are at right now. Do not look at what others are doing and become jealous. God has a special plan for your life and work that only you can do. Much of it will be behind the scenes where you never will get credit for it. You must be faithful in the small things before God entrusts to you the bigger ones.

How do you stay close to the Lord? Follow these steps.

1. Spend Time With God

Start with concentrated times with God every day. For some, it works best in the morning, and for others, it may be before you go to bed. It does not matter when during the day, only that you meet with Him.

2. Prayer

Talk to God throughout your day. Praise Him, pray in tongues, bring your needs before Him. Make Him a regular part of your life. How long would your marriage last if you only talked to your spouse for a few minutes every day and ignored them the rest of the time? Not very long. Prayer is between you and God, when you pray expect God to respond back to you. You talk He talks back and that is prayers.

Jesus is the lover of your soul, and He longs to be with you. Prayer is a two-way communication;

when you talk to God, wait until He talks to you; and tells you yes, no or wait.

3. The Word

Jesus is the Word of God.

> *In the beginning was the Word, and the*
> *Word was with God, and the Word was God.*
> *John 1:1 NASB*

If you want to know God, then you need to know His Word inside and out. If you have never read the entire Bible, now is the time. If you search online, you can find many reading plans to bring you through the Word in a year.

> *Your word I have treasured in my heart, that*
> *I may not sin against You.*
>
> *Psalm 119:11*

One of the best things I have done in my life is memorized Scripture and got it deep down into my heart. Memorize the Word. When I need it, God brings it to my memory for me to share.

4. Worship

Spend time recognizing and celebrating who God is. It can include music or not. It is an attitude of the heart that recognizes that God is God, and there is none above Him. Worship Him in spirit and in truth, by singing to Him, dancing to Christian music, etc.

5. Forgiveness

There are two aspects to forgiveness; first you must keep short accounts with God. Ask Him to forgive your sins regularly. Come before Him in repentance and humility, recognizing your need for a Saviour.

You must also be willing to forgive others. Offence is one of the ways that the enemy uses to divide the family of God. There will come a time when a brother or sister in Christ will hurt you and what you do that moment matters.

We are all human, and none is perfect except Jesus. We will make mistakes, and when someone does, you need to forgive them and let God come in and heal your heart. If you are holding offence, repent and ask for forgiveness, and God will heal your heart.

6. Go To Church

Have regular fellowship with your church family. Listen to Sermons and go to Bible Study. Develop strong relationships with believers that you can confide in and learn from them. Get involved with a local church, so your gifting and character can be developed.

Now Is The Time

I want to thank you for reading this book and allowing me to share my heart with you. I hope that this book has inspired you to live a life worthy of God filled with His supernatural power.

I love to move in the prophetic, prayer & miracles. It is an honour to serve the Lord in this way. If you are a Businessperson, Entrepreneur, Professional looking for Christian Coaching and building a business God's way, I would love to work with you.

If you are a Pastor or Church Leader and would like me to come to speak and minister in deliverance, healing, signs, wonders and miracles or could use help with church planting and growth, I would love to talk to you about it.

If you would like to connect with me for Coaching, Ministry, Speaking Opportunities or getting bulk copies of this book to share, please email me at zak@gariba.org, zkgariba@yahoo.ca, or you can visit my website at www.Gariba.org.

The Sinner's Prayer Or Confession Of Your Faith To Jesus

As a Christian it is referring to any prayer of repentance, prayed by individuals who feel convicted of the presence of sin in their lives and have the desire to form or renew a personal relationship with God through Jesus Christ. It is a popular phenomenon in evangelical circles to become born again Christian.

Christians see reciting the sinner's prayer as the moment defining one's salvation, others see it as a beginning step of one's lifelong faith journey.

It also may be prayed as an act of "re-commitment" for those who are already believers in the faith. Often, at the end of a worship service, in what is known as an altar call, a minister or other worship leader will invite those desiring to receive Christ (thus becoming born-again) to repeat with him or her the words of some form of a sinner's prayer.

The "Sinner's Prayer" takes various forms, all of which have the same general thrust. You can recite this to become a born-again Christian means a follower of Jesus.

The famous one I like is from Billy Graham

"Dear Lord Jesus, I know that I am a sinner, and I ask for Your forgiveness. I believe You died for my sins and rose from the dead. I turn from my sins and invite You to come into my heart and life. I want to trust and follow You as my Lord and Saviour. In Your Name. Amen."

Once you confess this or recite this you have become a follower of Jesus and you are a Christian or born-again Christian. The only time in God is now.

I want to end by encouraging you to stay strong in the Lord and in the power of his might (Ephesians 6:10). God has amazing plans for you (Jeremiah 29:11) and life in God is the only true life there is.

The Lord is my shepherd, I shall not be in want. He makes me lie down in green pastures, he leads me beside quiet waters, he refreshes my soul.

He guides me along the right paths for his name's sake. Even though I walk through the darkest valley, I will fear no evil, for you are with me; your rod and your staff, they comfort me.

You prepare a table before me in the presence of my enemies. You anoint my head with oil, my cup overflows.

Surely your goodness and love will follow me all the days of my life, and I will dwell in the house of the Lord forever.......

Psalm 23, NASB

Pastor Zak Gariba

A leader creates the atmosphere for people to follow, and when the leader leads, people's lives are changed. Leadership is not a popularity contest, as a leader leads in good times and bad times. People are looking for inspiration that speaks to their needs, the difference is leaders create winners. When leaders lead, people are challenged and motivated.

- Pastor Zak

Printed in Great Britain
by Amazon